HELP FROM
HEAVEN

ANDREA JO RODGERS

HARVEST HOUSE PUBLISHERS
EUGENE, OREGON

Cover design by Bryce Williamson

Cover photo © Mordolff / gettyimages

Interior design by Greg Longbons

Names and minor details have been changed in the real-life stories shared in this book to protect the
privacy of the individuals mentioned.

Help from Heaven
Copyright © 2020 by Andrea Jo Rodgers
Published by Harvest House Publishers
Eugene, Oregon 97408
www.harvesthousepublishers.com

ISBN 978-0-7369-8076-0 (pbk.)
ISBN 978-0-7369-8077-7 (eBook)

Library of Congress Cataloging-in-Publication Data is on file at the Library of Congress, Washington, DC.

Printed in the United States of America

20 21 22 23 24 25 26 27 28 / BP-GL / 10 9 8 7 6 5 4 3 2

This book is dedicated to Janine, Liam, Ciara, and Dylan Frawley (Frawley Strong) for their incredible strength, courage, and faith as they begin each day anew.

It is also dedicated in loving memory to my friend Heather Bray, whose unwavering faith and optimism glowed brightly for all who knew her.

Lastly, it is dedicated to my family as well as volunteer firefighters and first aid squad members of the past, present, and future.

· · · · · · · · · · · · · ·

Praise be to the LORD God, the God of Israel,
who alone does marvelous deeds.
Praise be to his glorious name forever;
may the whole earth be filled with his glory.
Amen and Amen.

PSALM 72:18-19

Acknowledgments

A special thanks to my proofreaders: Rick, Thea, and Katy. Thank you to my literary agent, Bob Hostetler, for his wisdom and support. Last but not least, a very special thank you to the staff at Harvest House Publishers and to my editor, Kim Moore, for her professional guidance.

Contents

Preface

The word "angel" comes from the Greek word *angelos*, which means messenger. Angels are referenced throughout the Old and New Testaments. They worship God and serve Him in many capacities. As ministers of God, they assist His people by providing protection and deliverance from danger. They can facilitate communication between God and His people via encouragement, revelations, and visions. They may act to guide and strengthen us. In certain instances, God may utilize angels to answer our prayers. They care for believers in their final moments on earth as they transition to the afterlife.

First responders have a unique opportunity to assist people in moments of crisis when they walk along a tightrope between heaven and earth. Sometimes, angels carry patients away to their ultimate destination. Other times, first responders may witness miracles in which people are protected and delivered from danger.

I've been blessed to volunteer as an emergency medical technician for more than 30 years and to work as a physical therapist for more than 25. *Help from Heaven* relates inspirational calls from my years on the rescue squad with biblical passages about angels. This book will explore the quiet ways our guardian angels may be close by our side in emergency situations.

Volunteer Members of the Pine Cove First Aid and Emergency Squad

Jessie Barnes—optometrist

Kerry Branson—architect

Dillon Chapman—college student studying to become a high school teacher

Mason Chapman—auto mechanic

Colleen Harper—college student studying to become a speech therapist

Archie Harris—retired state employee

Helen McGuire—nurse

Ted O'Malley—retired from a career in the national park system

Meg Potter—social worker

Andrea Jo Rodgers (the author)—physical therapist and a 30-year volunteer reflecting on first aid calls from her years on the rescue squad

Jose Sanchez—retired from a career in politics

Buddy Stone—retired pharmaceutical salesman

Greg Turner—electrical engineer

Alec Waters—special officer for the police department and a college student planning to become a veterinarian

Darren Williams—retired from a long career with the armed forces

Members of the Pine Cove Police Department

Officer Jack Endicott

Sergeant Derrick Flint

Dispatcher Jerome Franklin

Officer Jim Jones

Officer Kyle Jamieson

Officer Vinnie McGovern

Officer Brad Sims

Officer Fred Smith

Paramedics

Rose Anderson

Ty Fleming

William Moore

Paula Pritchard

Kennisha Smythe

Arthur Williamson

1

The Veteran's Second Chance

LORD my God, I called to you for help,
and you healed me.
You, LORD, brought me up from the realm of the dead;
you spared me from going down to the pit.

PSALM 30:2-3

The movie was quite enthralling, but now Lou Woodward was regretting that he and his wife, Carol, had gone. They'd had to park far from the theater, which hadn't seemed like a big deal before the movie, but by the time Lou got to the car after it was over, he was beginning to feel a tightening in his chest. *I wish I hadn't forgotten my nitroglycerin pills at home.*

"We really should get a handicapped placard. Between my hips and your bad heart, we certainly qualify," Carol said. Lou had suffered from angina for the past six years, and Carol had struggled with arthritis for about the same amount of time. They both knew she would have to get total hip replacements within the next year or two, but she was trying to put them off for as long as possible.

"No way are we getting handicapped plates. You know how I feel about that. That would mean we're getting old. Just the same, I think you'd better drive home, honey. I feel a bit out of breath." Lou plopped onto the passenger seat of their sedan, clicked his seat belt, and closed his eyes. *Just focus on taking nice, easy breaths. The chest pain will ease up, and I'll be home and able to take a nitro pill in 20 minutes.*

"Okay, but you are so stubborn about those handicapped tags. We *are* getting old, and you wouldn't be nearly so short of breath if you didn't have to walk so far." Carol put the car into gear and pointed it toward their home in Pine Cove, a beautiful seaside resort town on the East Coast.

"Maybe you're right. I'll think about it."

"Are you feeling okay, Lou? The fact that you're even considering those plates is scaring me, considering how dead set against them you are." Carol shot a concerned look at her husband, noting his pale, sweaty skin.

"I'm okay. Please just get me home." Lou briefly leaned his head against the passenger window before shifting it back to the headrest again. *This feels worse than my usual angina pains.*

Carol picked up the pace as Lou requested, edging her foot down on the accelerator. They both lapsed into a worried silence.

Lou was relieved when Carol pulled onto their driveway and nosed the car into the attached garage. He pushed open his car door and tried to swing his legs out, but they simply wouldn't cooperate. He suddenly found himself too weak to budge. "I think I'd better rest for a minute. Could you please run in and get my nitro?"

Carol rushed inside (as fast as a person with two arthritic hips could rush) and hurried back with Lou's small, dark-brown nitro container. She fished out a pill for him and watched as he placed it under his tongue. "I hope it helps. I'm really getting nervous. I don't think I can get you inside by myself. I'm not as strong as I used to be."

A few minutes passed, but Lou's chest still felt tight. *It's getting harder and harder for me to get air into my lungs.* "I think I'll try to stand up again." He used his arms to help swing his legs out of the car. Once his feet were on the ground, he pushed with all his might to stand up. However, he rose only a few inches before sinking down onto his seat again.

"I don't like this one bit. I'm going inside and calling the police department. They'll send us help."

Lou grunted in agreement and closed his eyes.

. . . .

DISPATCHER: "Request for first aid at 417 Hanover Road in the garage for a 77-year-old man with chest pains and difficulty breathing."

I initially joined the first aid squad back when I was in high school, more than 30 years ago. At the time I spent summers working as an office clerk at the beach. One hot summer day, Alec Waters, a special officer (aka beach cop) who volunteered with the Pine Cove First Aid and Emergency Squad, convinced me to join. I continued to answer calls during my college years (when I spent summers working as a special officer) and postgraduate years (while I studied to become a physical therapist). I feel blessed that I've been able to continue serving my community to this day, answering more than 8,000 first aid and fire calls.

"Looks like a detour is up ahead," Meg Potter said on our way to Hanover Road in the ambulance, noting a sign with some accompanying cones in the distance. Meg was a children's social worker. I admired her easy manner and ability to efficiently run a first aid call.

"I'll go around and approach Hanover from the other direction," Mason Chapman replied. "It looks like the road is torn apart, so we're definitely not getting through there." Mason, an auto mechanic at a local garage, helped us keep our ambulances in good working order.

After a brief delay, we arrived at the first aid call. An older woman, whom I assumed was our patient's wife, stood by the curb, waving her arms to attract our attention. After Mason pulled over, Meg and I grabbed our first aid equipment and joined her.

"I'm Carol Woodward. My husband is sitting in the car. I'm really worried about him. He's had chest pain before, but never like this."

We followed Carol up the driveway toward an attached two-car garage. I noticed that a large American flag flapped in the breeze close to the entrance.

Once inside, I glanced around the garage. The shelves were lined with the typical stuff, such as half-filled containers of windshield wiper fluid, old cans of paint, several green plastic watering cans, a rusty bicycle pump, and a can of WD-40. I squeezed between the wall and a maroon sedan, heading toward Sergeant Derrick Flint and Officer Vinnie McGovern.

Sergeant Flint was known for being both sharp witted and conscientious. "This is Lou Woodward, age 77," he said, pausing to look at his wristwatch. "He's been having chest pain now for thirty minutes. Pain is substernal, radiating to the left shoulder. He rates it a six out of ten."

"He also has shortness of breath, so we put him on a non-rebreather, fifteen liters. He took a nitro pill as soon as he got home, which was about five minutes ago," Officer McGovern said. He'd left his job as a corrections officer in South Carolina to join our police force. His brains, strength, and courage made him a great addition to the department.

"Hi, Mr. Woodward. I'm Meg, and this is Andrea and Mason. We're volunteers with the first aid squad."

"Thanks for coming," he replied. "I feel downright crummy."

Wordlessly, I handed Meg a blood pressure cuff.

"Your blood pressure is 90 over 60. Too low for you to take another nitro pill right now," Meg said. She slid a pulse oximeter monitor on his right index finger. "Ninety-six percent, but he's on oxygen." Normal pulse oximetry readings usually range from 95 to 100 percent without supplemental oxygen.

After jotting down the numbers on our call sheet, I slipped outside to find Carol. She was leaning on the garage's doorframe, lines of worry creasing her brow. "He's always gotten better with nitro. Do you think he's going to be okay?"

"He's holding his own right now," I replied, trying to strike a cautious balance between sounding reassuring and yet not overly confident he would be fine. "But we do need to take him to the emergency room. Can you tell me if he has any medical history or problems?"

"He has diabetes and high blood pressure. He's had angina for years, and he takes nitro when he needs it. I can't remember the name of his blood pressure medication, but I know I have it written down some-where." Carol rifled through the contents of her pocketbook. A few scraps of paper fell out of her purse, and I quickly stooped down to pick them up. "Oh, that one's it," she said, pointing to a folded index card.

I added the name of the medication to our call sheet. "Any aller-gies to medications?"

Carol shook her head. "Just to shrimp, but he didn't eat any fish today."

"Medics aren't available," Officer McGovern interjected. "I'll let you know if I hear otherwise."

"Thanks," I murmured, glancing toward the front of the car. Mr. Woodward was pivoting to the stretcher with help from Mason and Meg. Within a few minutes, he was loaded into the ambulance.

"I'll meet you at the hospital. I need to get a couple of things first." Carol hurried back toward the house, disappearing inside.

We loaded Mr. Woodward into the ambulance. Mason returned to the driver's seat, and Meg and I climbed into the back.

Lou sighed. "I should have skipped the movie. It was pretty good, but it wasn't worth going through all this."

"Well, you might have developed chest pains anyway. Maybe not today, but they could have caught up with you tomorrow," Meg pointed out.

"I guess I'm a little afraid of what the doc's going to find wrong with me. I didn't want to make a big deal out of it in front of Carol, but I know something's truly wrong. This feels different from my usual chest pains," Lou confided.

"It's good that you're going to get checked out." Switching topics to try to take his mind off his pain, I asked, "Have you been married a long time?"

"We got engaged right before I left for the Korean War. I married Carol a week after God brought me safely home."

I adjusted the pillow behind Lou's head. "That's so romantic. Has the chest pain gotten any better?"

Lou tapped his index finger against the center of his chest. "I'm afraid not."

"How's your breathing?" I glanced at the oxygen gauge to confirm he was still receiving 15 liters per minute.

"It's about the same. The oxygen seems to be helping a bit."

We arrived at the emergency room a few minutes later, with Lou still complaining of feeling "downright lousy." After Meg gave the report to the triage nurse, we said our goodbyes.

Just as we were leaving, Carol Woodward arrived. "Please keep us in your prayers," she murmured.

"We certainly will," I replied. I gave her hand a quick squeeze.

Dear Lord, You kept Mr. Woodward safe when he valiantly fought for our country. Please keep him safe again now.

. . . .

Four months later

Lou was looking forward to sitting down, but instead he stomped some snow off his boots and kept shoveling. *I'm almost done. The snow isn't very heavy. It's light and fluffy. I told Carol I'm not really shoveling. I'm just pushing the snow. No big deal. I'll concentrate on the driveway and leave the front sidewalk for later.*

After going to the hospital a few months earlier with chest pains, Lou underwent emergency surgery. The cardiac surgeon found three blocked vessels in his heart, so he went "under the knife" for a triple-bypass procedure. The doctor said eating too many cookies and potato chips had finally caught up with him.

After another ten minutes of shoveling, Lou knew it was time to throw in the towel. He felt oddly light-headed, as though his brain were beginning to swirl. *I'll get a glass of water. I hope I didn't overdo it. I'm doing so great in cardiac rehab.*

Lou leaned the snow shovel against the garage and stepped directly into the mudroom. Wearily, he sank down on the cedar storage bench near the coat hooks and began pulling off his boots. Halfway through pulling off the second one, he paused. "Carol, can you get me some water?"

Carol popped around the corner with a tall glass of water. "I still don't think you should have gone out there. Leave the shoveling for the young folks."

"Perhaps you're right. I hate to tell you this, but I feel strange. You know, light-headed. Like I'm starting to float."

"Do you feel as if you're going to faint? Now that you mention it, you look awfully pale. Should I get you an aspirin?"

Lou didn't answer. Instead, he slid off the bench onto the floor, landing with a thud on his left side. His mouth hung open, and he began making an odd gurgling noise.

"Lou, wake up! Answer me!" Carol shrieked. When he didn't respond, she grabbed the phone that hung just above the mudroom counter and frantically speed-dialed the local police department.

"Pine Cove Police Department. Dispatcher Franklin speaking. How can I help you?" Dispatcher Jerome Franklin had been with the Pine Cove Police Department for close to a dozen years. All the officers respected him for his knowledge, quick thinking, and dedication. They knew he had their backs.

"Help! My husband was shoveling snow and he's collapsed!"

"I'm dispatching the police and first aid right now. Please stay on the line," Dispatcher Franklin said calmly.

DISPATCHER: "Request for first aid at 417 Hanover Road for a man who collapsed after shoveling snow. Expedite."

Returning to his conversation with Carol, Dispatcher Franklin said, "Help is on the way. Can you tell if your husband is breathing?"

"I'm not sure. He's making a horrible gurgling noise."

"Do you know how to do CPR?"

"No, and I'm not sure if I can get down to the ground. I have really bad hips. But I'll try."

"I'll talk you through it. Just do your best."

"I'm putting you on speakerphone." Carol realized she had to pull herself together to help Lou. Grabbing the bench with one hand, she crashed awkwardly to her knees.

"Roll your husband onto his back if he's not already there. Push down on his forehead and pull up on his chin to open his airway. He might be making that gurgling noise because his tongue is blocking his airway," Dispatcher Franklin instructed.

"Okay, I did it. What next?" But before he could reply, there was a loud banging on Carol's door.

"Pine Cove Police," Sergeant Flint and Officer McGovern said in unison, entering the mudroom and springing into action.

"Thank God you're here!" Carol tried her best to stand up and get out of the way.

Sergeant Flint helped her up and then immediately dropped down onto his knees. Lou was taking ineffective, gasping breaths. "Agonal respirations. No pulse. Start CPR."

· · · · · · · · · · · · · ·

I had wondered from time to time when I drove past Lou Woodward's house how he had made out after the night we took him to the emergency room with chest pains. My heart sank when I recognized his address.

DISPATCHER: "Update: CPR is in progress."

"Received. Put us out at the scene," Mason said.

Meg and I exchanged worried looks. I recalled the last time we'd taken Mr. Woodward to the hospital and how touched I was by his devotion to his wife and country. *Don't think about that now. Just focus on bringing him back.*

When we arrived, Meg and I loaded our arms with the first aid jump kit, defibrillator, oxygen, portable suction unit, and patient clipboard and rushed up the driveway into their home.

Sergeant Flint glanced up at us as he performed chest compressions. "We hooked him up to the defibrillator and shocked him once already, but still no pulse."

"I told him not to shovel. It must have been too much for him. He's just getting over heart surgery." Carol's hands were clasped together as though in prayer.

I glanced up and saw Mason lead her away to ask more questions about exactly what transpired before she called us. *It's probably better that she doesn't watch. If he doesn't make it, I wouldn't want this to be her last memory of her husband.*

I measured an oropharyngeal airway (aka oral airway) from the tip of Lou's ear to the corner of his mouth and then carefully inserted it. An oral airway is a curved plastic device used to assist in maintaining the patency of the upper airway. In other words, it helps to keep the tongue from blocking the airway. "You can take over squeezing the BVM," Officer McGovern said, passing me the bag valve mask.

"The defibrillator is ready to analyze again. Hold compressions." We knew Lou must be in ventricular fibrillation (V-fib), a heart rhythm characterized by ineffective contractions of the heart (quivering) caused by abnormal electrical activity. Instead of regular, normal contractions, the heart was like a bag of squirming worms.

We all paused, making sure not to touch Lou to avoid getting accidentally shocked ourselves. "Shock advised," the machine said and began making a revving noise as it prepared to deliver a shock. I said a quick, silent prayer as Meg pressed the shock button.

"No pulse. Continue CPR," Sergeant Flint said.

Come on, Mr. Woodward. This isn't over yet. Hang on. Don't surrender. Fight!

The mudroom was warm, and I took a second to peel off my coat and toss it up onto the dryer. Meg followed suit, throwing hers on top of mine. Even though Carol was in a different room now, I could hear her crying softly. I couldn't imagine the terror she must be feeling. We continued CPR, pausing just long enough to roll Lou onto a backboard to prepare for transport to the hospital.

There was a quick knock on the door, and paramedics Arthur Williamson and Kennisha Smythe entered. Arthur, an experienced and insightful paramedic, was a great asset to us on first aid calls. Kennisha, soft spoken and levelheaded, helped ensure that calls ran smoothly.

I thought the pair made an excellent team. The tightly packed room grew even more crowded.

"Was it a witnessed arrest? What's his down time?" Kennisha asked.

I nodded. "Yes, his wife saw him collapse and started CPR. The police administered one shock with the defibrillator before we arrived, and we gave another shock just a minute ago. He's probably been down about ten minutes now."

I couldn't help but notice how incredibly bluish-purple Lou's face looked, possibly indicating that his blood wasn't being perfused with enough oxygen. *If we don't bring him back soon, he'll have permanent brain damage.*

"I'll intubate," Arthur said. Intubation is the insertion of a flexible plastic tube, known as an endotracheal tube, into the trachea (windpipe) to maintain an open airway.

Kennisha established an intravenous line. She switched him from our defibrillator to their own and intently studied his ECG. "He's still not in a shockable heart rhythm. Let's load him up and get going."

We carried Mr. Woodward on a backboard out of the mudroom and placed him onto the stretcher, which was parked by the garage door. While Sergeant Flint and Officer McGovern rolled the stretcher down the driveway toward the ambulance, Mason performed chest compressions and Meg squeezed the BVM to provide Lou with much-needed oxygen. I trailed behind, carrying as much equipment as I could.

The hands on the clock in the back of our ambulance showed no mercy, ruthlessly advancing. With each minute that ticked by, I knew Mr. Woodward's chances for resuscitation grew dimmer.

"I have V-fib on the monitor. Everyone clear," Arthur said. He placed the defibrillation pads on Lou's chest. Life-saving joules of energy surged though him.

"I have a carotid pulse. Can someone confirm?" Meg asked.

Kennisha placed her fingers on the artery at the side of Mr. Woodward's neck. "Yes, he definitely has a strong pulse. Hold compressions. Andrea, keep bagging him."

Okay, Mr. Woodward, you're halfway there. Your heart is beating again, but you need to breathe. I squeezed the bag valve mask, willing Mr.

Woodward to start breathing on his own. I watched with hope as the cyanosis on his face gradually faded, replaced with a nice pink color. "Mr. Woodward, your wife really loves you and needs you. I want you to take a breath for me." Because he was unconscious, I knew the odds were that he couldn't hear me. However, I hoped some part of him would understand my plea.

For a few long, painful seconds, there was absolutely no response from Mr. Woodward. Then miraculously, he suddenly drew in a life-saving breath. A deep, wonderful, all-on-his-own breath.

Arthur felt the artery near Mr. Woodward's wrist. "I have a good radial pulse now too." Next, he adjusted the intravenous flow. "Hang in there, Lou. We're on our way to the hospital."

The blanket over Mr. Woodward began to move. He was wiggling his feet! As I pushed the blanket out of the way to take a closer look, he reached for his face with his right hand.

"Sorry, Lou. That tube has to stay in," Kennisha said.

Meg gently stroked the top of Mr. Woodward's head. "Mr. Woodward, can you open your eyes for us?"

After a ten-second delay, just as we were pulling into the emergency room parking lot, his eyes popped open. Puzzled, he looked around the ambulance to try to figure out where he was.

"Everything's going to be okay. We're taking you to the hospital," Kennisha reassured him.

In my heart, I knew her words were true. *Everything's going to be okay.*

. . . .

Are not all angels ministering spirits sent to serve those who will inherit salvation?

HEBREWS 1:14

There are many references to angels throughout the Bible. As "ministering spirits," they tend to the needs of others. When Mr. Woodward was resuscitated in the back of our ambulance, I had no doubt he would return home with his wife and enjoy more happy years with her. Perhaps an angel stood by his side during the Korean War to bring him safely home. An angel may have held his hand during his open-heart surgery. At the direction of God, an angel may have been assisting us when Mr. Woodward regained his pulse and returned to his earthly life.

Thank You, Lord, for giving this veteran a second chance.

2

The Hit-and-Run

Send me your light and your faithful care,
let them lead me;
let them bring me to your holy mountain,
to the place where you dwell.

PSALM 43:3

Everett Bridges raised his glass to toast the newly engaged couple. "Rosie, words can't express how delighted I am for you and Antonio. Here's to a lifetime of love and happiness." He was thrilled his granddaughter had found such a nice young man to marry. They seemed extremely well suited and absolutely devoted to each other. He couldn't recall a time when he'd seen Rosie looking quite so radiant as she did tonight at the Coastal Cove Restaurant.

"Thanks, Grandpop. I'm so glad you could be here with us to celebrate," Rosie replied.

Everett had recently had a few health issues. Five months ago, he'd developed a blockage in one of his coronary arteries and had to get a stent. Three months later, he'd had a sudden onset of horrendous pain from several large kidney stones. Luckily, the pain had only lasted a few days. However, it had prompted him to make some real changes in his life. He'd started eating healthier and walking two miles a day. He was looking forward to becoming fit and perhaps staying out of the doctor's office.

"Yes, here's to the happy couple. I'm ecstatic for you," Everett's daughter, Audrey, said.

The next hour passed quickly with lots of laughter and reminiscing. "It's been a wonderful evening, but it's getting late. I think it's time for us to go." Audrey stood up and placed her napkin on the table. "I'll get the car and pull up to the front door for you, Dad."

"Now, don't be spoiling me. I'm perfectly capable of walking, you know. I've been exercising quite a bit lately," Everett protested.

"I know, but I'm afraid the parking lot may have a few icy patches, and I don't want to take any chances. I'll meet you outside just to the right of the front door." She dropped a kiss on his forehead and scurried out before he could try to change her mind.

Rosie and Antonio stood up and hugged Everett goodbye. Rosie then helped him put on his coat. "We're going to hang out a little longer. Do you want me to walk you to the door?"

"No, you two sit down and enjoy yourselves. Believe it or not, I still remember what it's like to be young and in love. I'll wait out front for your mother."

Everett wound his way through the large dining room, buttoned up his coat, and stepped outside under the covered entryway. He and Audrey had parked rather far away, so he waited on the curb, realizing it might take her a few minutes to get the car. In the distance, he saw a pair of headlights approaching. The headlights loomed closer, temporarily blinding him.

Everett tried to back away from the curb. In his haste, he stumbled and threw up his arms to catch his balance. Suddenly, a blinding pain ripped through him, and he felt himself being thrown high up into the air. Then, with a thud, he landed on something hard and cold. Terrified, he realized he must be on the hood of a car. He tried to scream, but no sound came forth.

Suddenly, the car was thrust into reverse, and he felt it moving backward. As quickly as the car was backing up, he felt the sudden switch of gears. The car lurched forward, swerving violently from side to side.

I'll never be able to hang on. Help!

. . . .

Audrey pulled her silver sedan next to the curb by the restaurant's awning. She didn't see her father, so she shifted into park and turned on the radio. After a minute or so, she decided to go inside to check on him. She retraced her steps to their dinner table, where Rosie and Antonio were still seated. "Where's Grandpop?"

Rosie sprang to her feet. "I helped him put on his coat, and then he said he'd walk to the door on his own. He isn't outside?"

Audrey shook her head. "No, he's not out there. Antonio, would you mind checking the men's room for us?"

"Of course not. Right away." Antonio walked toward the bathroom in the front lobby of the restaurant.

Audrey nervously twirled a strand of hair around her right index finger, unwound it, and then twirled it again. "I don't like this. If he's not in there, I don't know where in the world he could be."

Rosie squeezed Audrey's hand. "Don't worry, Mom. I'm sure he's in there. Where else would he go?"

Antonio reappeared, shaking his head. "He's not in there. Let's go check with the front desk. Maybe they know something."

. . . .

Rita Mays hummed along with the radio, tapping her thumbs on the steering wheel in time with the beat. As she rounded a curve, she saw a mound in the middle of the road. Hitting the brakes, she threw her car into park and put on her hazards.

The road was dark, and she squinted as she walked toward the mysterious object. As she drew closer, she realized with burgeoning horror that it was a person. She rushed back to her car and dug her cell phone out of her purse. With trembling fingers, she dialed 911.

"Nine-one-one. What is your emergency?" the dispatcher asked.

"I need an ambulance. I'm near the Coastal Cove Restaurant. A man is in the middle of the road, and it looks like he's been hit by a car. He's not moving at all. I don't know what to do."

. . . .

DISPATCHER: "Request for first aid near the Coastal Cove Restaurant for a pedestrian struck. Expedite."

Buddy Stone jumped onto the driver's seat. One of our longtime members, he had recently retired from his job as a pharmaceutical salesman and was now able to devote more time to answering first aid calls. Ted O'Malley quickly climbed onto the passenger seat next to him. Retired from a career in the national park system, Ted was another longtime first aid volunteer.

Helen McGuire climbed into the back with me. "I just got off work," she said, still sporting her light-blue nursing scrubs. Despite working long shifts as a nurse, she still somehow managed to find time to volunteer for the squad.

A few minutes later, Buddy slowed down as we approached the Coastal Cove Restaurant. The road was closed to traffic, and a police officer from a neighboring town moved a traffic cone to allow us to pass through. "It looks like the scene is straight ahead. I'm going to park here," Buddy called back to us.

We swiftly gathered the trauma kit and necessary equipment and rushed to the victim. Sergeant Flint was kneeling next to the patient, carefully stabilizing his head and neck. "We're trying to figure out exactly what happened," he said grimly. "I think perhaps he was crossing the road and was hit by a car, or he fell first and then was accidentally run over. Possible hit-and-run. We got an ID from his wallet. His name is Everett Bridges."

The older-looking gentleman lay on his side, his eyes closed. The lenses of his glasses were shattered, and blood was dribbling from his nose and mouth. His right hip was turned unnaturally outward, indicating that it was possibly fractured.

Helen began a head-to-toe examination. I took over holding cervical stabilization from Sergeant Flint so he could join the accident investigation team. As I glanced after his retreating figure, I noticed a lone shoe farther down the road, close to the gutter. I looked down at our patient's feet. One of his shoes was missing. It was hard to tell from where I was, but it looked as if it might be a match. *If that's his shoe, he may have been thrown quite far by the car. No wonder he's in such poor shape.*

Ted placed the gentleman on high-flow oxygen, carefully adjusting the mask's strap just above his ears and around the back of his head. Then he placed a cervical collar around the patient's neck.

"He has deformity of the right shoulder and leg. He's unresponsive with a Glasgow score of 5," Helen said. The Glasgow Coma Scale is an assessment tool for trauma patients to help figure out how severe an acute brain injury is. Scores range from 3 to 15, with 3 being the worst possible score and 15 the best.

"What did you get for a pressure?" Buddy asked, patient clipboard in hand.

"Blood pressure is low…96 over 50. Heart rate 112. Let's get him on the backboard," Helen said.

Suddenly, I heard sobbing and the sound of footsteps drawing closer. I looked up and saw three distraught faces. "Dad, is that you?" a middle-aged woman with shoulder-length brown hair asked. She grabbed my elbow. "What's happening to him? Why is my father in the middle of the road?"

When Sergeant Flint realized that family members had arrived on scene, he came over to speak with them. "Ma'am, we're trying to figure that out right now. We thought perhaps your father was crossing the road. Did he park his car somewhere over here?"

The middle-aged woman, whom I later learned was Audrey, knelt next to her father. "No, no. He was supposed to be waiting at the entrance. I went to get the car. I didn't want him to have to walk out here in the cold. And now look what's happened."

Sergeant Flint strode over to the covered entryway, with the younger two family members following close behind him. Audrey stayed with us. "Is he going to be okay?" she asked.

"We're doing everything we can to help him. We're taking him to a trauma center," Helen replied. "The paramedics from the hospital will be here within a minute or two. They'll start an IV line for your father and give him any medications he may need."

Sergeant Flint reappeared a moment later. "I found this brown hat at the entranceway. Do you know if this belongs to your father? Your daughter isn't sure."

"Yes, that's his. What do you think happened?" Audrey asked.

"I saw tire marks on the curb. I'm sorry to say this, but it's starting to look as though your father was involved in a hit-and-run accident. Excuse me for a moment. I need to get this on the air right away."

I realized Sergeant Flint wanted neighboring towns to start looking for a car with front-end damage.

Audrey turned to Buddy and me. "Is he saying that someone hit my father in front of the restaurant? Then why is he here, all the way down the street?"

I was silent for a moment. Sergeant Flint's implication wasn't pleasant. Audrey's father either may have been on the hood of the car before eventually falling off, or perhaps he was dragged underneath the vehicle for a distance before somehow shaking loose. Either alternative seemed dreadful.

"Someone hit my dad and dragged him all the way here? And never even stopped? Who on earth would do such a terrible thing?" Audrey asked.

The question hung in the air for a moment. "Unfortunately, sometimes people do terrible things," Helen murmured.

As we hoisted Everett into our ambulance, paramedics Rose Anderson and William Moore arrived. Rose began assessing him while William listened to Helen's report. Rose flashed a small penlight into his eyes, trying to gauge whether his pupils were equal and reactive to light. "Right is dilated and nonreactive," she said, briskly moving along with her assessment.

"We're going to need to intubate and sedate him," William said.

Rose perched on the edge of her seat, which was close to Everett's head. After William sedated him, she carefully laced an endotracheal tube down his throat to keep his airway open. "Can you check my tube placement?"

William placed his stethoscope in numerous places on Everett's chest and abdomen, listening for lung sounds as Rose squeezed the bag valve mask. "Good placement on the tube," he said. "Andrea, you can take over for Rose and start squeezing the bag. Nice and easy. Don't hyperventilate him."

I began squeezing the BVM as instructed, watching as the air gently inflated Everett's lungs. Using a sterile gauze pad, I wiped a small amount of blood from the corner of his mouth. *This poor man. His entire life has changed in the blink of an eye, all due to some other person's reckless driving.*

William shook his head. "He appears to have a severe brain injury and possible internal injuries. That hip and shoulder could be broken too. We'll head straight into a trauma bay when we arrive at the hospital."

Helen and I nodded. We knew the drill. The next hours would prove critical to Everett's survival.

．．．．．．．．．．．．．

A few days later

Everett Bridges. I held the physical therapy orders in my hand with a mixture of hope and apprehension. The orders stated that he was in the surgical intensive care unit. I figured he probably had surgery for his hip, shoulder, or maybe other internal injuries. After reviewing his medical chart, I took a deep breath and knocked on the glass door to his room.

"Come in," a female voice said. As I entered, I recognized Mr. Bridges's daughter, Audrey. She rose to her feet and drew closer.

"Hi, my name is Andrea. I'm a physical therapist here," I said.

"Thanks for coming. I'm not sure how much my dad will be able to do today. He was in a really bad accident a few days ago."

Audrey didn't recognize me, and I didn't expect her to. The accident scene had been dark, and she'd been traumatized by the events that had transpired. I briefly explained that I was a volunteer with the rescue squad, and that I'd been with her father that horrible night.

A frown creased Audrey's forehead. "Did you know they caught the guy?"

"No. Did they track him down after the accident?" I knew they'd been diligently searching for the hit-and-run driver.

"Within an hour. Drunk as a skunk. He claims he didn't even realize he hit my father. How can you hit a person, have him hang off your hood for almost a block, and not even notice?"

I didn't have an answer for her, though I knew it was a rhetorical question. She just needed to vent. All I could hope was that justice would eventually be served. It would be up to the courts now.

"They found him after he had crashed into a couple of trash cans in an alleyway, passed out behind the wheel. The cops knew he was the guy because a piece of my dad's coat was caught in the fender, and the windshield was cracked."

"How's your father doing?" I could see he was still intubated and sedated, hooked up to a ventilator that was breathing for him. It made a constant *whoosh* noise, almost hypnotic in nature.

"Not so great. He hasn't woken up yet. The night of the accident, the surgeons had to cut open his skull to take some of the pressure off his brain. Yesterday, he had surgery to fix his broken right arm and leg, and he pulled through that okay. He has a severe brain bleed and a skull fracture."

I knew the arm and leg would heal with time, but brain injuries are trickier. After I asked questions about Everett's life before the accident, I checked his range of motion and skin integrity. He had bruising and swelling around his eyes, and his head was shaven on one side where the surgeons had operated. I taught Audrey how to gently range her father's arms and legs. "Because he can't move himself right now, it'll help if you can do this for him. It'll prevent his joints from becoming stiff."

I continued to see Everett every couple of days after that, though he remained unresponsive. Then about a week later, his eyes were open, and he was off the ventilator. Audrey met me at the door, smiling brightly. "I'm finally starting to get my dad back. I think he understands what I'm saying. He can wiggle his toes when I tell him to."

When I stepped into the room and squeezed Everett's hand, he returned my squeeze. My heart filled with hope that he would be blessed with a full recovery.

. . . .

He will command his angels concerning you
to guard you in all your ways;
they will lift you up in their hands,
so that you will not strike your foot against a stone.

PSALM 91:11-12

At God's direction, angels provide protection and deliver us from danger. Everett could easily have died from the accident, but by the grace of God he lived. As I worked with Everett, he began to assist with simple range-of-motion exercises. I knew it would only be a matter of days before he would be discharged to a rehab facility. He would have a long and difficult road, but I had faith that he would ultimately do well.

3

Swept Away

Save me, O God,
for the waters have come up to my neck.
I sink in the miry depths,
where there is no foothold.
I have come into the deep waters;
the floods engulf me.
I am worn out calling for help;
my throat is parched.
My eyes fail,
looking for my God.

PSALM 69:1-3

There's no parking. None. I'm going to have to lug my beach chair and all my stuff four long blocks. Why didn't I get here sooner?

Stephanie Bradford had slept late and enjoyed a leisurely breakfast before deciding on the spur of the moment to head to the shore. Now, faced with the prospect of parking so far away, she wished she'd gotten an earlier start to her day. She finally found a space on Wesley Avenue. Slinging her backpack over one shoulder and her beach chair over the other, she grabbed her small cooler with her right hand and began the hot trek toward the beach.

Stephanie's left arm began aching after about three blocks. She'd had rotator cuff surgery five months earlier for a partial tear of one of her muscles, and she wasn't 100 percent back to her old self yet. She placed the chair, cooler, and backpack down on the sidewalk and rested for a few minutes. Then she heaved her gear back into her arms, made her way along a narrow path that led to the boardwalk, and struggled down a flight of wooden stairs to the sand, pausing to inhale the crisp, salty air and enjoy the refreshing sea breeze.

Eventually she trekked toward the water, close to the lifeguard stand. She preferred sitting near the water, but the beach was very crowded. Slowly, she began meandering south, farther away from the guard stand. After about a block, she found an open area where she could set up her chair and lay down a beach towel.

Stephanie plopped into her chair, took a long swig of ice-cold water, and closed her eyes. After drowsing for a half hour or so, she felt hot. The cool sea breeze had died off, and she decided to take a dip in the ocean. *I know I'm not near the guards, but other people are swimming here, too, so it's not like I'll be alone. I'll just go in up to my waist and get right out again.* She was a decent swimmer, but she preferred to swim where her feet could touch the bottom.

Stephanie smiled at another young woman who stood at the water's edge. She slowly inched her way into the waves. Initially, the water felt unpleasantly cold, but then she gradually got used to it and decided that it felt quite comfortable.

Close to a dozen people swam and splashed in the water around her. Stephanie eased herself onto her back and closed her eyes, enjoying the sensation of gently floating over the waves. She lost track of time and suddenly opened her eyes with a start.

Stephanie tried to put her feet down on the ocean floor but realized with dismay that she couldn't touch the bottom. Although she was close to the shoreline, the fact that she couldn't touch the bottom made it seem like she was far away. A thread of fear took root within, but she firmly brushed it aside. *I'll just swim in to where the other people are.*

But when she looked more closely at the shoreline, she realized that the other swimmers were gone. Her initial quiver of unease now blossomed into outright panic. She tried her best to swim back toward the beach, but her shoulder ached. She realized she really wasn't making any headway. No matter how hard she tried, she didn't seem to get closer to the shore.

Stephanie was a low-key kind of person who didn't like to attract attention to herself. But at this moment, she desperately wanted to attract the entire world's attention. She realized if she didn't get help soon, she would be in deep trouble. Raising her right hand above her head, she cried out as loudly as she could. She grew increasingly exhausted, and it became harder and harder to keep moving her arms and legs. *Help me, God.*

. . . .

DISPATCHER: "Request for first aid near the Wesley Avenue Beach for a person with heat exhaustion."

Summer calls for heat exhaustion on the beach are as common as fireflies on a warm summer's night. Alec Waters, Mason Chapman, and I had just returned from the beach a few minutes earlier, where we had responded to a first aid call for a young man with abdominal pain from heat cramps. We helped him into the shade, and he drank a bottle of cold water. Because he didn't want to go to the hospital, he signed a refusal form (which people suffering from heat-related emergencies often do). Now, it looked as though our crew was heading directly back to the beach again.

Alec, who was currently in school to become a veterinarian, was the person who initially convinced me to join the first aid squad. Both incredibly smart and kind, he was a great asset to the community. "Looks like round two," he said, heading back toward the ambulance.

"I can drive this time if you want," Mason said. He checked us in service, and we headed east once more.

"It's going to be a bit south of Wesley Avenue. Patrols on scene advise that the patient fainted," Dispatcher Franklin told us.

"Received. We're just about on location now." Mason maneuvered the rig into the yellow zone close to the beach entrance. Knowing that we would probably be met with another refusal, we rolled the stretcher as far as the boardwalk and carried the rest of our equipment across the sand.

We found our patient, Sally, sitting under a large green-and-white-striped beach umbrella. She was sipping a bottle of cold water that one of her friends had given her. With her long dark hair pulled back in a ponytail, she looked to be no more than 20. "I'm okay, honestly," she said, clearly embarrassed by the attention. "I'm going to drink this water, and then my friends are going to take me home."

Alec checked Sally's blood pressure and pulse, while I placed a cold pack behind her neck. Mason drenched a towel with cold shower water and draped it over her shoulders to further cool her off.

I handed Sally our refusal form, which she promptly signed.

"Please call us back if you change your mind," Alec said.

. . . .

Hearing some sort of commotion behind her, Terri Cromwell put down her book and took off her headphones. She noticed several emergency medical technicians (EMTs) on the beach tending to a young woman who looked like she had heat exhaustion. Digging into her cooler, Terri pulled out an ice-cold soda and took a long swig.

She glanced out at the water, mesmerized by the way the waves crashed on the shoreline, one after the next, as part of a never-ending cycle. Suddenly, a movement just beyond where the waves were breaking caught her attention. Unsettled, she stood up. She gazed intently at the spot where she thought she had seen something unusual. *Nothing. There's absolutely nothing there. My eyes are playing tricks on me.* And yet, she couldn't shake off the sense of disquiet that filled her.

She glanced toward the left and noted that the beach chair where the young woman with the pretty auburn hair had been sitting was empty. Terri had been so focused on her book that she really hadn't paid much attention to the people around her. Acting on an almost automatic level, she found herself walking over to an older gentleman sitting to her right.

"Excuse me," she began, nervously running a hand through her tangled hair. "I know this sounds crazy, but I thought I might have just seen something out there, but now I don't see it. Have you noticed anything unusual?"

The man immediately jumped to his feet, dropping his small bag of mini pretzels in the process as he gazed toward the ocean. "No, but then I haven't really been paying much attention."

"There's an empty beach chair next to me, and I'm not sure where the woman is who was sitting there. Of course, now my imagination is running away with me. It's probably nothing, but what if...?"

"Honestly, I think you should tell a lifeguard right away," he replied. "I'll stay here and keep watching that spot until you get back. Maybe it's nothing at all. And then again, maybe you truly did see someone who needs help. Let's err on the safe side."

"Okay, you've convinced me. I'll go tell a guard." Turning abruptly, Terri began running toward the lifeguard stand as quickly as she could. *It's probably nothing, but I could never live with myself if I really did see a person out there and didn't do anything about it.*

. . . .

Just as Mason, Alec, and I were starting to walk back toward the boardwalk, I heard lifeguard whistles. Pausing to see what was happening, the three of us turned toward the water. Lifeguards sprinted from numerous directions, heading to a spot near the water not far from where we now stood.

"I wonder what's going on," I said.

Alec put down our first aid bag. "It looks like we better hang out here for a minute before we head back."

Mason nodded in agreement. "They might need us." As soon as he uttered the words, our pagers were activated.

DISPATCHER: "Please stand by at the Wesley Avenue Beach for a report of possible swimmer in distress."

Mason pulled a portable radio out of his pocket. "We're on location. We're clear from the last call. It was an RMA." (RMA stands for "refused medical attention.")

The three of us quickly headed across the sand, closer to the water's edge. "I can't see any swimmers in the water," Alec said. "Maybe they already pulled someone out." But as we reached the water, I could see that the lifeguards were forming a line straight across the shore and entering the surf. I figured that by staying close together, they must be increasing the odds they would find the person.

"Someone thought they may have seen someone in distress, but they weren't sure," I overheard one bystander say to another.

Is someone out there? If so, the poor person is already under water. The lifeguards will have to painstakingly search until they come across him or her.

A few minutes passed, and the crowd of observers grew accordingly. It seemed as though the group was collectively holding its breath, unsure of what the outcome might be. Hushed murmurs swept through the onlookers as each person relayed the story to the next.

Suddenly, one of the lifeguards shouted, "I have someone!" Several of them pulled the person's head above the water's surface and began working their way toward the shoreline.

I quickly cranked our oxygen bottle to 15 liters while Alec finished setting up the bag valve mask. Seconds later, the team of lifeguards dragged a young woman with long hair toward us. Her face was a ghastly shade of gray, while her lips were white. *She looks as though she may have been under for a while.*

We got to work. "She's got a weak carotid pulse, but she's completely unresponsive," Alec said. "Let's get her on her side and see if we can get some of the water out."

"Another rig already called in service. I'll radio them to bring the suction unit down here," Mason said.

The young woman lay completely motionless on her back, her eyes closed. But as soon as we rolled her to her side, she began retching water.

"One of the cops said he thinks her name is Stephanie Bradford," a lifeguard said. "He's trying to confirm it right now. He's checking the ID found in a bag by an empty beach chair close to where she was found."

"Stephanie, it's going to be okay. We're taking you to the hospital." I hoped she might hear my words on some level and be reassured, even though she was unconscious.

Although her eyes remained closed, Stephanie began thrashing her arms and legs. I hoped it was a sign she was regaining consciousness.

"The paramedics are ten minutes out. They're responding from Bakersville Hospital," Mason said.

Stephanie's coughing eased, and she grew still. Then, unexpectedly, she opened her eyes and sat bolt upright. "What happened? Who are all of you?"

With those two gloriously lucid questions, I knew Stephanie was going to be okay. We transported her to the hospital, and she went on to make a full recovery.

. . . .

Peter was kept in prison, but the church was earnestly praying to God for him.

The night before Herod was to bring him to trial, Peter was sleeping between two soldiers, bound with two chains, and sentries stood guard at the entrance. Suddenly an angel of the Lord appeared and a light shone in the cell. He struck Peter on the side and woke him up. "Quick, get up!" he said, and the chains fell off Peter's wrists.

Then the angel said to him, "Put on your clothes and sandals." And Peter did so. "Wrap your cloak around you and follow me," the angel told him. Peter followed him out of the prison, but he had no idea that what the angel was doing was really happening; he thought he was seeing a vision.

ACTS 12:5-9

This scene in Acts 12 demonstrates that God may answer our prayers via the actions of angels. Stephanie made a desperate plea to God for help, and many people on the beach were also praying for her. Thanks to an alert bystander, an outstanding team of lifeguards, and a first aid crew who happened to be in the right place at the right time, all the pieces fell neatly together as God orchestrated the remarkable rescue of one of His children.

4

I Want to Stay Home

God is our refuge and strength,
an ever-present help in trouble.
Therefore we will not fear, though the earth give way
and the mountains fall into the heart of the sea,
though its waters roar and foam
and the mountains quake with their surging.

PSALM 46:1-3

Pain exploded in Margaret Bergman's right hip like fireworks on the Fourth of July. She heard an ominous, loud cracking noise and knew instantly that she'd just broken her hip. *No, please no. Not now. Not like this.*

Margaret slowly rolled off her stomach and onto her left side. *Just take some deep breaths. Get hold of yourself.* She managed to push herself up onto her left elbow and peek down at her leg. Then she wished she hadn't. Her right foot was turned outward much farther than normal.

I have to call my sister. She'll know what to do. However, the phone was down the hallway, on the coffee table in the living room. *It might as well be a mile away across a hot, sandy desert.*

Margaret knew there was no point in yelling for help. She lived in an upstairs garage apartment, and there really weren't any neighbors who lived close enough to hear her. The couple who owned the main house on the property was away on vacation. Plus, a fierce blizzard with howling winds was currently burying the town of Pine Cove in snow, so she knew that no one was around to hear her cries for help. Anyway, Margaret wasn't quite sure if she wanted anyone to hear her. She was extremely private and tended to keep to herself. In fact, she rarely left the safety of her apartment. *I wonder if someone could come and just put a cast on me here, so I wouldn't have to leave.* With determination, she began to painstakingly slither on her belly toward the telephone.

. . . .

I squirmed uncomfortably, the metal bar on the narrow cot at the first aid building digging into my right hip. I switched to my other side, but it didn't help much. I startled for the umpteenth time when the furnace made an odd moaning noise reminiscent of a prowling tomcat on a hot summer's night. *Just give up. You're never going to get to sleep.*

As it turned out, I didn't have to keep trying.

> **DISPATCHER:** "Request for first aid at 689 Chambers Street for a 66-year-old female with seizures."

I jumped to my feet, slid into my snow boots, and grabbed my heavy winter coat. A few seconds later, I met Ted O'Malley and Jessie Barnes in our first aid building's second-floor hallway.

"I just looked out the window. There's already at least eight inches of snow on the ground. It's going to be tough to get there," Jessie said, moving quickly toward the stairs. An optometrist in a nearby town, he spent much of his free time volunteering as an EMT with the Pine Cove First Aid Squad.

Ted zipped up his heavy winter coat. "Good thing we decided to stand by at the building."

"It definitely would have been tough to make it here from home," I agreed. Normally, since all our squad members live close to the first aid building, we respond to emergency calls from our houses. Tonight, however, we decided to stay at the building in case the storm prevented us from being able to travel there safely.

Jessie climbed into the driver's seat, flipped on the emergency lights, and pulled onto the building's concrete apron. "It's even worse than I thought. It's going to be really rough going."

I watched as snowflakes piled up onto our windshield almost faster than the wipers could chase them away. "Let's hope we make it there safely." There had been several occasions in which a whole bunch of us had to push the rig when it got stuck in snow, and it was usually a memorable (but not super fun) experience.

"In service," Jessie told the dispatcher, cautiously pulling out onto the road. The howling wind created swirling clouds of snow, severely limiting visibility.

"Be advised, your patient is now conscious and alert," Dispatcher Franklin responded. *At least if we get into trouble, it's comforting to know that Jerome's only the push of a radio button away.*

The ambulance slid a few feet in protest as we rounded the corner onto Chambers Street. "It's hard to see house numbers with all this snow, but I guess it's the house with all the lights on," Ted said.

Jessie pulled up in front of a two-story stucco home with a large front veranda. We then lugged our first aid equipment through the snow. I accidentally bumped a low-hanging evergreen branch, which promptly dumped a pile of snow on my shoulders.

Officer McGovern arrived and joined us as we entered the home. "It could be pretty tough to carry her out." He stopped to stomp large clumps of snow off his boots onto the front mat before following us in.

A harried-looking gentleman with short, curly gray hair and old-fashioned glasses, which perched precariously on the edge of his nose, rushed downstairs to meet us. "Hi, I'm Hank Boggs. I'm so terribly sorry to drag you out in this. My wife, Tina, started seizing, so I called 911 right away. She's doing much better now. Please follow me." He paused at the last step, then promptly turned around and headed back upstairs again.

We hastened after Hank, though I made sure to hold the handrail in case my wet boots slipped on the hardwood. We followed him down a short, brightly lit hallway to the second room on the right.

A middle-aged woman lay in the middle of a king-size bed, a dark burgundy comforter covering her from the waist down. Her cheeks were flushed, and her eyes were bright with unshed tears. "I'm so embarrassed. I can't control the seizures. They always seem to come at the worst time. I feel awful that you had to come out in this terrible storm for me."

"So, you've had seizures in the past?" I fished a blood pressure cuff out of our first aid bag.

"Yes, I've had a few each year since I got in a bad car accident ten years ago and suffered a brain injury. I recovered, but I still have seizures."

I reached across the bed and wrapped the blood pressure cuff around Tina's upper arm. "Well, at least you were in bed and didn't fall."

She sighed. "Yes, that's happened before. A few years ago, I fell and broke my shoulder from a seizure. Some people get an aura that indicates the seizure is coming, but unfortunately, I don't. It's always very sudden. I'm just glad that Hank was here with me."

I finished taking her blood pressure and pulse. "BP is 122 over 76 and heart rate is 74," I said to Jessie, who was writing up the report.

"Would you like to go to the hospital?" Ted asked.

"No thanks," Tina politely declined. "I want to stay home."

"We have an appointment with her neurologist tomorrow. I'll keep an eye on her tonight. I hate to say it, but we're used to this routine," Hank said.

"Call us back if you change your mind," I said. Jessie handed her our call sheet, and Tina signed our refusal form.

"I promise, we will," Hank said. "And I hope you make it safely back to your station."

DISPATCHER: "Request for first aid at the rear of 821 Waverly Drive for a hip injury."

"That's our cue to leave. We have another call. We're glad you're okay." Jessie grabbed the first aid bag and headed for the door.

I briefly shook Hank's hand and then followed Jessie and Ted back out to the ambulance. "We've got a refusal here, so we'll be responding directly to Waverly Drive," Jessie said to Dispatcher Franklin.

"Received," Dispatcher Franklin replied. "Patrols are advising that the patient is in a garage apartment. I'm dispatching the fire department to assist you with manpower."

Great idea. If the person needs to go to the hospital, we could use more hands to help with lifting and shoveling. I fastened my seat belt and held my breath as our rig slogged slowly through the heavy snow.

Jessie gripped the steering wheel tightly. "It looks like another half inch has fallen just while we were inside." The light from the streetlamps reflected off the snow, making it appear oddly bright despite the late hour.

"Oh good, there's a snowplow ahead of us. Maybe we can follow him toward Waverly Drive," Ted suggested. The snowplow operator must have heard the first aid call on his radio, because he plowed a path for us all the way to our next call. I've learned over the years that every member of the team—official or unofficial—plays a crucial role, coming together to help those in need. This was clearly one of those cases.

About ten minutes later, we parked in front of a small white Colonial on Waverly Drive. At least, it looked like it was white. Everything at that moment looked white with all the snow.

"I don't think I'm going to be able to back down that driveway," Jessie said. "It's too steep and narrow. Not to mention, it's buried in snow. We'll have to carry the person out to the road."

I nodded in agreement. "Yes, it's too risky to try backing down the driveway. We might slide or get stuck. And those low-hanging branches might scratch the top of the rig."

Once Jessie had parked, Officer Jack Endicott worked his way down the driveway to meet us. He was following in his family's footsteps; he came from a long line of distinguished police officers. "I don't think you need an X-ray machine for this one. Based on her pain level, the cracking noise she heard when she fell, and the way her foot is turned outward, she most likely has a hip fracture."

As Ted and I gathered equipment to splint the fracture, a fire engine pulled up behind us. Chief Ray Watson and his crew stepped out.

Chief Watson had volunteered on the first aid squad with us for several years, but he had resigned to devote his time to the fire department when he was elected fire chief. "Glad to help you in any way we can," he called out, smiling despite the storm. "You just tell us what you need."

"Thanks," Jessie said. "We'd sure appreciate it if you could shovel a path up to the door for us as well as the flight of outdoor steps to the upstairs apartment."

Chief Watson nodded, and he and his fellow firefighters grabbed snow shovels. Jessie, Ted, and I headed up the long driveway to the detached garage at the rear of the property. The snow was getting high, and I felt a chunk of it slide inside my boot and down along my sock.

We trudged up a flight of wooden steps to the second floor, and Jessie knocked briefly before swinging open the door. An older woman with shoulder-length gray hair lay on the floor with her back propped up against a beige couch. I could see right away that Officer Endicott was correct; her right foot was turned outward, signaling a possible hip fracture. My gaze swept from her foot up to her face. I could see the look of pain in her eyes but realized that there was something more than that. *Pure, unmitigated terror.*

I knelt close beside her. "Hi, I'm Andrea, and this is Jessie and Ted. We're with the Pine Cove First Aid Squad. What's your name?"

"Margaret," she whispered, her voice barely audible.

"Can you tell me what happened tonight? Did you pass out when you fell?" I was trying to determine if she had experienced some sort of medical event that had led to her fall or if she had simply tripped or lost her balance.

Margaret grabbed hold of my hand and pulled me close, so close that our heads were nearly touching. She looked me straight in the eyes. "I don't leave my apartment very often."

I hesitated for a moment, not sure of how to respond. "You don't like to go out much?"

"I guess I'm what some people might call a recluse. I haven't been out much over the past few years. My sister goes shopping for me. I like it here. It's…well, it's safe." A tear hung briefly on the edge of her eyelashes before slowly sliding down her cheek. "It's broken, isn't it? I can tell just from looking at it. And it hurts so much. I'm going to have to go to the hospital, aren't I?"

"I'm so sorry. You definitely have to go to the hospital. The doctor will want to take X-rays." I didn't add that she might need surgery. They could break that news to her in the emergency room. At her age, if she had surgery, she might need to go to a rehab center for a week too. She probably wouldn't be coming back home anytime soon. I gently patted her shoulder, hoping to bring her some small measure of comfort but unsure if I could.

Margaret's shoulders slumped in defeat. "I knew that's what you were going to say. I called my sister, but she can't get here because of all the snow. She's the one who called 911." She took a deep breath. "Okay, do what you need to do. I really just want to stay home, but I'm going to have to deal with it, I suppose."

"We'll talk you through it the whole way," Ted said kindly. "There are also some firefighters outside shoveling a path for us. In a few minutes, they'll come in and help us lift you out to the ambulance."

Margaret struggled for composure, casting her eyes downward. "Thank you."

After taking a set of vital signs (blood pressure, pulse, and respiratory rate), we used a scoop (a type of stretcher that separates into two pieces lengthwise) to immobilize Margaret's hip. Chief Watson and his crew members helped us lift her up and carry her toward the door.

This poor woman. What a dreadful way to suddenly be thrust back into society. A bunch of strangers in her home, dragging her out of her comfort zone into a raging snowstorm. Then the promises of a nail-biting drive to the hospital. After that, it'll only get worse. More strangers, more questions, a bunch of tests, and perhaps even surgery. What a terrifying ordeal.

The door to the outside flew open, caught in the fierce wind. At that moment, Margaret left the safety of her small garage apartment. Not by choice. Not on her own two feet. Instead, she left on a hard-plastic scoop carried by four strong men. And in that moment, she left her life as a recluse both physically and symbolically as she was thrust across the threshold into the ferocious and frightening outdoors.

· · · · · · · · · · · · · ·

Two days later

As I arranged my physical therapy orders for the morning, one name caught my attention. *Margaret.* I scanned down the order sheet and discovered that she had undergone surgery for a hip fracture.

I'd thought about Margaret a lot since the first aid call two nights ago. I wondered how she was holding up, propelled out of her safe cocoon and into the medical world. Now I would have a chance to see firsthand.

A little while later, after reviewing her medical chart, I knocked on the door to her room. *Will she be okay? Or will she be cowering in her bed, terrified of the world?*

"Come in," a voice called out. It sounded friendly and strong.

I stepped past the curtain and leaned the walker I had brought against the wall. "Hi," I said, smiling brightly. Margaret was sitting up in bed, a magazine in her lap and her breakfast tray pushed off to the side.

"Oh, hi. You're the girl from the other night, aren't you?" she asked, smoothing back a few stray strands of gray hair.

"That's me. I'm happy to see you're looking so well. How are you?"

"Well, as you can see, I had to have surgery. All things considered, it went well, I think. Everyone has been very kind. And now that the roads are clear, my sister was able to visit."

I placed a bedsheet on the light green recliner next to her bed. "Would you like to try getting up and walking to the chair?"

Margaret smiled. "That sounds great. I'm going a bit stir-crazy lying here."

After evaluating Margaret's range of motion and strength, I helped her sit on the edge of the bed. With a small boost, she was able to stand up and, using the walker, take a few steps to the recliner.

"That was terrific! Is the plan for you to go home or head to rehab from here?" I asked.

"I'm not sure yet. The doctor said it depends how I do with physical therapy. If I'm able to walk with a walker, I can go home, and my sister can stay with me. You know what?"

"What?" I asked, amazed by her strength of spirit and resiliency.

"This whole experience hasn't been nearly as bad as I thought it was going to be. Everyone's been so wonderful." Margaret chuckled. "Maybe I should have broken my hip years ago."

. . . .

Last night an angel of the God to whom I belong and whom I serve stood beside me and said, "Do not be afraid, Paul. You must stand trial before Caesar; and God has graciously given you the lives of all who sail with you." So keep up your courage, men, for I have faith in God that it will happen just as he told me.

ACTS 27:23-25

When we are frightened, angels may encourage us. Margaret was able to overcome her fear of leaving her home. Perhaps an angel of the Lord was holding her hand through the whole experience. God gave her the courage to reenter the adventure of life.

5

A Different Kind of Angel

Many are the woes of the wicked,
but the LORD'S unfailing love
surrounds the one who trusts in him.
Rejoice in the LORD and be glad, you righteous;
sing, all you who are upright in heart!

PSALM 32:10-11

Frank Pendleton's eyes popped open, and he glanced at his small, old-fashioned windup alarm clock. *Just what I thought. Time to get up.* Pushing back his navy-blue comforter, he swung his slim legs over the edge of the bed and pushed himself up into a sitting position. His head buzzed for a few seconds, but he determinedly shook off the queasy feeling that threatened to envelop him.

"Good morning," Doris Pendleton, his wife of 40 years, greeted him as she entered the room. "Are you feeling any better today?" She leaned over and placed the back of her hand on his forehead. "It doesn't feel like you have a fever."

"I feel about the same. I'm glad you made that appointment with Dr. Creed for this afternoon. Something's not quite right, but I can't put a finger on it. The dizzy spells seem to come out of the blue." Frank slid his feet into his fuzzy plaid slippers and took a sip of water from the glass on his night table.

Doris placed a kiss on Frank's cheek. "I'm going to run to the grocery store and pick up a few things. I have to get gas and stop at the bank too. I'll be back in a bit."

"I'm sure I'll be fine. I'm going to take a shower and eat some breakfast. Could you please pick up one of those delicious crumb cakes from the bakery?" Frank stood up, briefly grabbed the corner of the night table to steady himself until the dizziness passed, and shuffled toward the bathroom.

Thirty minutes later, after a shower and shave, he decided to make fried eggs and toast. He grabbed his empty water glass and headed toward the staircase. A sudden wave of dizziness struck just as he stood on the top step. Frantically, he tried to grab onto the railing to steady himself. Despite his efforts, he collapsed and was only dimly aware that he was falling into a pit of darkness.

A short time later, Frank slowly opened his eyes and struggled to recall exactly what had happened. Then it all came cascading back…feeling faint and blacking out. He could tell from the sight of the small table in their foyer that he must have fallen down the entire flight of stairs to the first floor.

Tentatively, Frank tried to wiggle his fingers and toes. Even though he could move them, he knew he'd never be able to get up without help. In fact, he didn't think he could get up even *with* help. He felt like something was wrong with his neck and shoulder, and his lower leg as well. After what seemed like an eternity—but was probably only about ten minutes—Frank heard Doris's car pull onto the driveway.

· · · · · · · · · · · · ·

DISPATCHER: "Request for first aid at 620 Kensington Avenue for a fall victim down a flight of stairs. The patient is alert and conscious at this time."

Alec Waters, Darren Williams, Archie Harris, and I responded to the call. When we arrived at the address, Archie asked, "Hand me a pair of large gloves, would you?" Retired from the state government,

Archie had been volunteering with the Pine Cove First Aid Squad for many years.

"Okay, if the shoe fits. I mean, if the gloves fit," Darren joked as he tossed a pair of medical gloves to Archie. Darren had retired after a long career with the armed forces. He used much of his free time to answer our daytime first aid calls.

Sergeant Flint was just stepping out the front door as we were stepping in. "You're about to be tapped out for a possible stroke. Do any of you need a ride back to the first aid building to get another rig?"

"Yes, thanks," Alec said. "Darren and I will go back with you. Archie and Andrea can handle this one." He turned around and followed Sergeant Flint to his patrol car.

Archie looked to me and smiled. "It's you and me now, kid. I guess those gloves better fit after all." He stooped to pick up the first aid bag Alec had placed on the front porch.

We found our patient as soon as we stepped through the door. An older gentleman lay crumpled at the bottom of a steep flight of oak steps. I glanced upward; the thin floral runner that ran the length of the stairs probably hadn't done much to soften his fall. Shards of glass lay on the ground near his legs.

Archie recognized the victim right away. "Hey, Frank. What happened?"

"Oh, hi, Archie. Nice to see a familiar face. I think I must have blacked out. Thanks for coming to help me out," Frank replied.

A frazzled-looking woman with short blond hair hovered near Frank. "I got home from running some errands, and it was a terrible shock to find him sprawled out on the ground like this. I should never have left him alone."

Frank tried to comfort his wife. "Doris, I'm sorry I gave you such a fright. Everything's going to be fine. Please stop worrying."

Doris explained how Frank had been feeling under the weather, and they had an appointment with Dr. Creed scheduled for that very afternoon. "I guess I better cancel that. I bet we'll still be at the hospital."

Archie carefully avoided pieces of glass as he squatted down next to Frank. "Does anything hurt?"

"My neck is killing me, and my right shoulder feels like it might be broken. My right leg's not feeling so hot either. It looks like I did it good this time."

"Where did all this glass come from? It looks like it cut up your leg," Archie noted.

"I was carrying an empty glass downstairs. I must have dropped it when I passed out. Please be careful. I'd feel terrible if you cut yourselves."

Officer Brad Sims approached us and said, "I'll grab the collar and backboard from the rig." Officer Sims made an imposing figure at six foot three. He was a huge help to us with lifting patients, and I was glad he was here today.

"Hi, Mr. Pendleton," I said. "I'm with Archie. My name is Andrea. How's your breathing?"

Frank paused to consider. "Not too bad. I mean, it's been better, but it's not terrible."

Frank's pulse oximetry reading was 92 percent, so I pulled a nasal cannula out of our respiratory bag. "I'm going to give you a bit of oxygen. It should help you feel a little better." After I placed the short prongs of the nasal cannula in his nose and looped the tubing around his ears, I slid my hand over his wrist, feeling for a radial pulse. *I can't feel a radial. That means his blood pressure must be very low. No wonder he passed out.* "Do you know what your blood pressure normally is?"

"It's been running sort of low lately, I think," Frank replied. "Doris, do you know?"

"Yes, I took it yesterday, and it was 100 over 68. That's low for Frank. I just bought one of those take-it-yourself units at the drugstore last week."

I wrapped a blood pressure cuff around Frank's left upper arm and inflated the cuff. "BP is 78 over 50," I said. Archie jotted it down on our patient clipboard.

By the time we completed our assessment, placed a cervical collar around Frank's neck, put a sling around his shoulder, bandaged and splinted his leg, and placed him on a backboard, paramedics Arthur Williamson and Kennisha Smythe arrived from the hospital. "Since you already have him all packaged up, we'll get him loaded and start an IV line in the rig," Kennisha said.

The trip to Bakersville Hospital was largely uneventful, and we passed the time with small talk. "I have a bad feeling that I'm going to be laid up for a while," Frank said ruefully.

Kennisha adjusted the drip on the intravenous line. "Well, bones mend. It just takes time."

"We're pulling up to the emergency room now. You'll be in good hands," I said.

Frank grabbed my right hand with his left and squeezed it firmly. "God bless you."

Three little words, but such a thoughtful thing to say. *How kind of Frank to be thinking of me right now, instead of focusing on himself and his own injuries.* "Thank you. And you as well."

. . . .

A week later, our rescue squad responded to a first aid call a few doors down from the Pendletons' house. While I was lifting the cot out of the ambulance, Mrs. Pendleton came over to say hello.

Most times, we never get to find out what happens to our patients after we drop them off at the hospital. Eagerly, I asked, "How's your husband doing?"

"Oh, I guess you could say he's an angel now," Doris replied.

I was momentarily shocked speechless. I could practically feel the color draining from my face. *Poor Mr. Pendleton's dead? Why sure, I know he had some serious orthopedic injuries. But I certainly never thought he might die. He seemed okay in the back of the ambulance. He was in a lot of pain, but he seemed to be holding his own.*

"I'm so sorry. I had no idea," I said.

Mrs. Pendleton smiled. "Oh, not like that. When I said that he's an angel, what I meant was that he has a halo now. You know, he has to wear a halo vest."

Actually, I had no idea what she was talking about. At the time, I wasn't a physical therapist yet and had never even heard of a halo vest. "I'm sorry. I'm not sure what you mean."

"Well, Frank fractured the second bone in his neck when he fell," she said.

"Oh, that's awful! Can he move his arms and legs?" I asked.

"Yes, thank God. The fracture didn't affect his spinal cord. The only way the surgeon could stabilize his spine was to put on this medieval-looking thing called a halo. It has a ring that goes around his head, which is how it got the name 'halo.' And it has these horrible spiky-looking pins that come out from his head, with bars that go down to his shoulders and attach to a plastic vest."

I mentally cringed at the image. "Is he in a lot of pain?"

"Surprisingly, no. And to tell you the truth, the halo's really a blessing. Frank doesn't need surgery. And with the halo, he's able to get up and walk. With help, of course. He fractured his arm too, and he has a bad bruise on his knee. He's at a rehab hospital now."

"Well, thank you for the update, and please send him best wishes for a speedy recovery," I said, glad that she had taken the time to let me know how her husband was doing.

"Yes, I don't want to keep you any longer, but I recognized you out the window and thought you might be curious as to how he made out. Please give Archie our thanks as well."

· · · · · · · · · · · · ·

He had a dream in which he saw a stairway resting on the earth, with its top reaching to heaven, and the angels of God were ascending and descending on it.

GENESIS 28:12

I was glad to hear Mr. Pendleton was doing relatively well, considering the severity of his injuries. He'd truly had a close call. Thank goodness the fall hadn't resulted in him climbing the stairway to heaven as described in the above verse from the book of Genesis. I was relieved I'd misunderstood Doris and Frank hadn't "earned his wings" yet after all. *He's a different kind of angel!*

6

Quacking Up

In my alarm I said,
"I am cut off from your sight!"
Yet you heard my cry for mercy
when I called to you for help.

PSALM 31:22

When a strange crackling noise slowly penetrated my subconscious, I roused myself from sleep and sat bolt upright in bed. A second later, my first aid pager went off.

> **DISPATCHER:** "Request for fire department and first aid on the 300 block of Meade Street for a working structure fire. Exact location to be determined."

I couldn't believe it. I lived on Meade Street! I yanked open my bedroom curtain. Angry orange flames shot straight up from the second floor of my neighbor's home down the street. The pungent smell of smoke filled my nostrils as it pushed its way through my window screen. I could hear frantic yelling and shouting in the distance.

I raced into my parents' room to wake them up. "Come quick! The Allens' house is on fire." Without waiting for a response, I rushed downstairs and outside. Although I'm not a firefighter, I raced over to see if I could help. (Side note: As a first aid squad member, I'm a firm believer in running away from burning buildings rather than running toward them. I'd rather let our brave firefighters bring the victims out to us. Of course, this case warranted an exception.)

Fortunately, I found the Allens outside of their home, standing by the side of the road. At the time, one of our neighbors was a paid city firefighter. Like a true hero, he'd already banged on the Allens' door and made sure that they got safely out.

The power of the flames was relentless. I watched in horror as the fire devoured much of the second floor within the span of a mere minute or two. Almost immediately, the fire department and first aid squad arrived. I checked in with our rig and let them know the homeowners were okay.

Our town's volunteer firefighters are top-notch. They quickly extinguished the flames, salvaging the rest of the home. We later learned that the fire had apparently started in a second-floor light fixture. Although the house was severely damaged, no lives were lost. That day reaffirmed my utmost respect and admiration for our firefighters. But it was at a fire call a few weeks later in which they truly endeared themselves to me.

· · · · · · · · · · · · · ·

DISPATCHER: "Request for fire department and first aid at 349 Shady Grove Lane for a general fire alarm activation."

I hopped into the front passenger seat of the ambulance next to Darren Williams.

"Let's roll. It'll probably be a quick one," he said.

I fastened my seat belt. "Yeah, hopefully it's a false alarm."

Darren turned up the volume on the radio just in time for us to hear Dispatcher Franklin say, "Nothing showing at this time."

"In service." Darren shifted the rig into drive, flipped on the overhead lights, and headed toward Shady Grove Lane.

DISPATCHER: "Update: Owner reports setting off the alarm in error. Roll easy."

As we wound our way closer to the scene, I shifted a bit and suddenly sat bolt upright as something outside the driver's side window caught my attention. "Stop the rig!"

Obviously unsure of why I was yelling, Darren slammed on the brakes. Not wasting a second, I jumped out and raced around the front of the ambulance toward the storm drain next to the curb. I dove toward the drain but was too late. Before I could stop him, the last of five tiny golden ducklings fell between the slats of the grate and down into the drainage pipes. The mother mallard stood anxiously nearby, appearing shocked that her precious babies were no longer next to her.

Darren rolled down his window. "What in the world are you doing?" he called to me from the ambulance, throwing me a look that suggested I might be certifiably insane. Ignoring the question, I knelt next to the drain and tried to pull up the grate. But no matter how hard I tried, I couldn't budge it. It was simply too heavy for me.

I'll briefly digress to note that I love ducks. I mean, I really *love* ducks. It all began when I was in the first grade. While my brother was working on a Boy Scout project at the park, he rescued a mangled baby duck. For me, it was love at first sight. Over the course of several days, my mom nursed it back to health and brought it to a wildlife rehabilitation specialist. The experience inspired me to write my very first "book" at the age of seven.

"Didn't you see those baby ducks fall down the drain?" I asked Darren. As I slowly rose to my feet, my mind searched for a solution to the dilemma.

"No, but you need to get back in the rig. We have to go to this call. We can come back afterward," Darren replied.

"It's a false alarm. The ducks need us more," I grumbled. *What if the ducklings are injured? What if they get swept away by the time we get back?* Indecisively, I looked at the despondent mother duck and then back at the storm drain. I could see the five ducklings all huddled together at the bottom.

I shifted my gaze. The fire trucks were just around the bend in the road. It was hard to tell, but it looked like the firefighters were already packing up their equipment. "Great idea—let's get there right away. I can ask the firemen for help."

As soon as Darren pulled up to the scene, I jumped out and ran over to Chief Watson. Briefly, I explained the situation.

"Lead the way. We'll follow you there directly."

Within two minutes, we were back at the storm drain. With a mighty heave, Chief Watson and another firefighter, Paul, successfully removed the heavy metal grid. Paul lay flat on his stomach and reached into the drain. One at a time, he carefully lifted each baby out and counted, "One, two, three, four."

"Uh-oh. There were five," I said. One tiny duckling was missing. *There's no way I'm leaving one behind. We have to find him.*

Standing back up, Paul brushed some dirt off his turnout gear. "We can trace the path of the drainage pipe. It must go under the road."

Much to my relief, we found where the pipe dumped into a small basin area. There, just a few feet from the end of the pipe, was baby duckling number five.

I lit up with joy. Suddenly, I was reminded of the parable of the lost sheep from Luke 15 as Paul reached into the drainpipe and carefully retrieved the last baby. To a chorus of rousing cheers from onlookers and squad members, he carried the little duckling across the street and reunited him with his family.

. . . .

The LORD God had formed out of the ground all the wild animals and all the birds in the sky. He brought them to the man to see what he would name them; and whatever the man called each living creature, that was its name.

GENESIS 2:19

In Genesis, we learn that God created all the creatures of the earth and sky. By giving them to man to name, he demonstrated we are responsible for them. To this day, saving the baby ducks ranks as one of my very favorite fire calls in which a group of us worked together as a team to rescue a family.

7

Turning Thirty

When I am afraid, I put my trust in you.
In God, whose word I praise—
in God I trust and am not afraid.
What can mere mortals do to me?

PSALM 56:3-4

Jenna Wharton had been looking forward to this weekend getaway
at a guesthouse in Pine Cove for months. She'd been running on
empty for weeks, struggling just to keep afloat. *My life is collapsing like
a deck of cards, and the joker is having a field day at my expense.*

She sank into a rocking chair and stared sightlessly out the window toward the stunning grove of pine trees, unable to appreciate their
beauty. She reflected on the last few months and groaned.

First, her landlord had found out she was illegally keeping a cat in
her apartment, so he'd served her with eviction papers for breaking the
terms of her lease. She could have stayed if she had given up her feline
buddy, but she couldn't part with her. Next, the solar company she'd
worked for had announced they were downsizing and subsequently let
her go. A few weeks after that, her boyfriend of five years had invited
her to a fancy restaurant for dinner. She had thought he was going to
ask her to marry him, but instead he'd dumped her.

She hated the thought of having to start all over again: figuring out where to live, where to work, how to meet Mr. Right. At the age of 29, the prospect of moving back in with her parents was hardly appealing.

After losing her job, Jenna began having anxiety attacks. The first one, which happened while she was home watching a movie, caught her totally by surprise. When her heart rate skyrocketed, she thought she was having a heart attack. An ambulance took her to the hospital, and she underwent a battery of tests. Nevertheless, the doctor couldn't find anything wrong.

"Have you been under stress lately?" the emergency room physician had asked. When she responded with a resounding yes, he diagnosed her with anxiety, prescribed Xanax, and advised her to follow up with her primary care physician and a cardiologist. Jenna intended to do so, but she just hadn't gotten around to it yet.

She had several more attacks after that, although a bit milder in nature. One occurred while she was driving to the grocery store, and another happened while she was taking a walk. They always seemed to come without warning, leaving her feeling frightened and helpless. *This weekend I'm going to relax, de-stress, and just focus on enjoying some peace and quiet.*

Determined to take her mind off her problems, Jenna pulled a fashion magazine out of her overnight bag to peruse. The strategy worked, at least for a little while. But ever so gradually, she began to feel the now all-too-familiar sensation that her heart was racing. She put the magazine down and closed her eyes, willing her heart to slow down. The uncomfortable feeling persisted. She tried taking some sips of cold water and even walked around the room to see if that might help. Unfortunately, it didn't. If anything, she was beginning to feel worse.

I don't want to call 911. I've already been to the hospital, and I'm sure it's just anxiety. So why can't I control it? Unsure what to do, Jenna perched on the edge of the queen-size bed. Her hands began shaking, and she couldn't catch her breath. Her chest was pounding, and she felt like she might pass out. She held on for another 15 minutes, hoping the feeling would go away. Instead, she continued to feel worse. Reaching for her phone, she reluctantly dialed 911.

. . . .

> **DISPATCHER:** "Request for first aid at the Evermore Guesthouse for a 29-year-old woman having an anxiety attack."

We tend to get lots of calls for patients suffering from anxiety attacks. These calls occur at all times of the day and night throughout the year. In fact, we received one just yesterday for a middle-aged man who had been suffering from anxiety attacks for the past 15 years. When the attack didn't ease up after a half hour like it usually did, he decided to go to the hospital to get checked out. "I'm at that age where I'm never quite sure if it's anxiety or if it's my heart," he explained.

"Seems to be a lot of stress going around lately," Colleen Harper remarked. Colleen, a speech pathologist, was one of my mentors when I first joined the rescue squad. I admired her ability to stay calm and levelheaded in emergency situations.

"True enough. Sometimes, I feel like anxiety is an epidemic," Mason Chapman replied.

"Yes, going hand in hand with depression," I added. It amazes me how many people report a history of anxiety as well as depression when we ask them about their past medical issues.

"Something tells me this isn't how this person wants to spend her vacation," Colleen said as we pulled up in front of the Evermore Guesthouse, a stately, turn-of-the-century Victorian.

Grabbing our equipment, we climbed a steep flight of steps to the large, wraparound front porch. I didn't have time to admire the cozy honey-oak porch swing or the beautiful palm plants that surrounded it.

The guesthouse owner, an elderly woman with long grayish-white hair held back with a jeweled hair clip, met us at the door. "Upstairs, room 207. Follow me." We followed her up the narrow, winding rear set of stairs to the second floor, which led us directly to the room we were looking for. "I'm going to give you privacy," the owner said. "I'll be downstairs if you need me for anything." She discreetly disappeared down the stairs.

Mason placed our first aid bag near the doorway. "We'll need the stair chair to get her down from here. I'll get it, and you two can start the assessment."

Our patient was a slim young woman with wavy blond hair pulled back into a high ponytail. She stood briefly when we entered but then quickly sank back onto the edge of her bed. "Hi, I'm Jenna. I'm really sorry to bother you. I'm having an anxiety attack that just won't ease up."

"I'm sorry to hear that. What time did the episode start?" Colleen asked as she passed me the patient clipboard so I could write down the information.

Jenna glanced at her wristwatch. "I guess it's been a half hour at this point. I feel plain lousy. My heart is racing, and my chest hurts. I feel dizzy and lightheaded, like I'm going to pass out."

Colleen placed her fingers onto Jenna's wrist to check her pulse. "How's your breathing?"

"It feels tight, like it's hard to get the air in. I know I should slow my breathing down, but I can't." Jenna slid farther back on the bed, nervously running a hand through her ponytail. I could see sweat glistening on her forehead and cheeks, so I jotted the word "diaphoretic" on the call sheet.

"The heart rate is so rapid that I can't quite count it. Can you pass me the pulse ox?" Colleen asked.

I quickly pulled it out of our kit and handed it to her. My eyes widened when I saw the heart rate reading of 250. A normal heart rate is 60 to 100, and a count of 250 is downright dangerous.

"Let's get you lying down," Colleen said smoothly. She helped Jenna swing her legs up onto the bed.

"Can you tell me what kind of past medical history you have?" I asked.

"I broke my arm when I was five. There's really nothing else I can think of besides anxiety."

I wrote down her response. "How long have you been suffering from anxiety?"

"It's been a couple months now. I guess you've probably heard it all before. I lost my apartment, my job, and my boyfriend. Not exactly how I dreamed my life would be when I turn 30 next month. I wish I could control the attacks, but I can't. They come on without warning," Jenna explained.

I patted her sympathetically on the shoulder. I knew things were bound to turn around for her, but it might take some time. "Do you take any medications?"

"Just Xanax when I need it. I took one when the attack started, but it hasn't done a bit of good yet, except to make me feel tired," Jenna replied.

"Does this feel like one of your typical anxiety attacks?" I asked, troubled by Jenna's high heart rate coupled with her other symptoms.

"Actually, it's a lot worse. That's why I finally decided to call 911 and get checked out. I hate to seem like a wimp, but…"

"You did the right thing by calling us," Colleen assured her. "Always follow your instinct. Your body is telling you that something isn't right." Turning toward me, Colleen said, "Her blood pressure is high, 164 over 96."

Mason reentered the bedroom, followed by paramedic team Ty Fleming and Paula Pritchard. Ty, a passionate advocate of emergency medicine, was taking prerequisite science classes in hopes of getting into medical school. His dream was to become an emergency room physician. Paula, formerly a preschool teacher, had recently decided to change careers and become a paramedic.

"Glad you're here," Colleen said. She briefly explained Jenna's condition.

"Hello, Jenna," Mason said. "We're going to check you out. For starters, I'm going to put you on our heart monitor to see exactly what your heart is doing. If you have any questions as we go along, please ask."

After the leads were attached, Paula and Ty studied the ECG on the monitor. "It looks like SVT," Paula said.

Ty nodded his head in agreement. "Jenna, we're going to start an intravenous line and give you some medication that should help you to feel better."

"Wait a second. Are you saying this is more than just an anxiety attack? What's SVT?" Jenna asked.

"SVT stands for supraventricular tachycardia. The electrical system of your heart isn't working right," Ty said.

"And it's making my heart race?"

Ty deftly prepared the IV. "Yes, that's right. Paroxysmal supraventricular tachycardia can cause you to feel anxious."

"So, it's not just because I'm stressed out?" Jenna asked.

"Well, SVT can be caused by many different things and can occur for unknown reasons. Emotional stress can sometimes play a role," Paula said.

Jenna closed her eyes. "And you think this medication will work? I feel terrible."

"I certainly hope so. It's an antiarrhythmic drug that's designed to convert your heart rhythm back to normal," Ty replied.

I held my breath as Ty pushed the drug into Jenna's IV, hoping that the adenosine would work for this poor woman. I kept my eyes glued to the heart monitor. Within a few minutes, her heart rate fell all the way down to 100.

Paula studied the ECG tracing. "Feeling any better yet?"

Jenna smiled. "Yes, much better. Thank you."

After that, we were able to help her sit up and get onto our stair chair so we could carry her downstairs.

"You know, the ER doc told me to follow up with a cardiologist, but I didn't. Now I really wish I had. Some of the episodes that I brushed off as anxiety could actually have been this SVT thing," Jenna said.

To be sure, this hadn't turned out to be a very restful vacation for Jenna. However, I felt like she was fortunate to get some answers and assistance for her medical condition.

. . . .

[Elijah] lay down under the bush and fell asleep.

All at once an angel touched him and said, "Get up and eat." He looked around, and there by his head was some bread baked over hot coals, and a jar of water. He ate and drank and then lay down again.

*The angel of the L*ORD *came back a second time and touched him and said, "Get up and eat, for the journey is too much for you." So he got up and ate and drank. Strengthened by that food, he traveled forty days and forty nights until he reached Horeb, the mountain of God.*

1 KINGS 19:5-8

These verses demonstrate that angels can provide us with direction, strength, and sustenance. After losing her job and boyfriend, Jenna was under tremendous stress. She needed guidance, strengthening, and encouragement. In her time of need, she recognized the importance of calling for medical assistance. Perhaps an angel, beckoned by the Lord, carried her through the ordeal.

8

On the Fence

Hear my cry for mercy
as I call to you for help,
as I lift up my hands
toward your Most Holy Place.

PSALM 28:2

Abe Martin sighed as he reached into the gutter, picking out a clump of muddy leaves and tossing it to the ground. He was wearing gardening gloves, but the dampness from the wet leaves had soaked through, leaving his hands feeling cold and stiff. He found himself wishing he'd cleaned out the gutters earlier, before it had snowed several inches. Usually, his wife, Mabel, held the bottom of the ladder for him, to make sure it stayed steady. The ground on the side of the house was uneven in certain spots, and he wasn't a big fan of climbing ladders, even on level ground. Unfortunately, Mabel was sick in bed with a cold, so he was on his own.

Abe climbed down, shifted the ladder over two feet, and climbed back up. His left knee ached, but he tried to ignore it. A few days ago, while he was walking his basset hound, he'd slipped on a wet sidewalk and twisted his knee. He figured it was just a strain, so he'd been putting ice on it regularly. He wasn't in the habit of going to the doctor, so the thought of getting his knee checked out by a physician hadn't crossed his mind.

He finished cleaning out the stretch of gutter at the front of his home and then moved the ladder around to the side of his house, alongside the family room. *I wish we had more evergreens and less deciduous trees. Maybe then we wouldn't have so many leaves.* Wearily, he climbed back up again and began dreaming about a nice cup of hot tea and some warm biscuits.

Suddenly, Abe's left knee buckled, causing him to lose his balance. The ladder began swinging backward, away from the house. Frantically, he tried to throw his weight forward and reach for the gutter. However, the ladder slid violently on the damp ground, and he found himself sailing backward, away from his home and toward his wooden picket fence.

His back slammed hard against the old fence, and he felt the wooden boards crumble under his weight. With a loud thump, he struck the ground and felt the air whoosh out of his lungs. For one long moment he simply lay there, too startled and in too much pain to move. With the ladder on top of him and the fence squashed beneath him, he wasn't even sure if he could move.

His eyes traveled down toward his toes as he tried to take stock of his situation. His gaze was drawn almost magnetically to his left arm, at which point he realized why he was in such horrific pain. A shard of the picket fence was sticking clear through his upper arm!

Abe realized his chances of getting up on his own were officially zero. He hoped Mabel would wake up and hear his cries for help.

. . . .

"Dwight, did you just hear that noise?" Fran Hawkins asked her husband while laying down the colorful scarf she was knitting on her lap. Fran volunteered her time with a local knitting group, which made hats and scarves for the less fortunate.

Dwight looked up from his crossword puzzle. "What noise? I didn't hear anything."

Fran tucked a loose strand of curly brown hair behind her ear. "I'm not sure. A thumping noise, I think. Like something fell." She stood up and moved to the front window, briefly pulling aside the curtain.

"Well, I don't see anything. I guess I imagined it." She sank back onto the couch and began knitting again.

A minute passed. Suddenly, Fran jumped to her feet. "I think I hear someone yelling for help."

"Are you sure? You mean from outside?"

Fran threw a sweater around her shoulders. "It must be. Let's take a look."

Dwight hustled out the front door. "I hear it now too."

The voice grew louder and appeared to be coming from their side yard. "Oh my!" Fran exclaimed, catching sight of the collapsed wooden fence.

Dwight rushed to his neighbor. "Abe, are you okay?"

"I'm so glad you heard me. I'm in a bad way. My arm…"

No more words were necessary. Fran took one look, and the blood drained from her face. "I'm going to call for an ambulance."

. . . .

DISPATCHER: "Request for first aid at 214 Shelton Avenue for a man impaled on a fence."

My mom paused from kneading her Irish soda bread batter. "Impaled on a fence. That sounds horrible. I hope the poor person is okay."

"Me too," I agreed, rushing out the back door. By the time I got to the first aid building, Dillon Chapman was already driving our rescue ambulance onto the front apron. Dillon, who had recently volunteered overseas as a missionary, was now studying to become a high school teacher. He was a great role model with his excellent EMT skills and a wonderful bedside manner. He was the second cousin of Mason Chapman, which is why these two squad members shared the same last name.

Ted O'Malley arrived at the same time as me and hopped into the front seat of the ambulance while I jumped into the back of the rig.

Mentally, I tried to figure out a game plan for how we might be able to help our patient.

Dillon pulled up in front of a gray two-story Colonial with field-stone trim. I noticed right away that Officer McGovern and three other people stood on the west side of the house, close to what remained of an old-looking wooden fence. As we drew closer, I could see a ladder lay across the grass, with its end resting on top of the remains of a crushed section of the fence. Just underneath the ladder was an older gentleman, his face contorted with pain.

Officer McGovern turned toward us. "This is Abe Martin. The ladder isn't putting any weight on him, so I didn't want to try to move it until you arrived. I was concerned it could set off some sort of chain reaction and move the fence, which could affect his arm. The medics aren't available."

A long shard of wood stuck straight through the upper part of Abe's left arm. I was briefly reminded of the fake arrows that people sometimes wear over their heads, to make it look like the weapon is piercing their skull. *Only this time, it's for real.*

"Thanks for coming," Abe managed to say. "How bad does it look?"

"Well, the good news is that the piece of fence that's going through your arm isn't attached to the rest of the fence anymore," Dillon said. "That'll make it much easier to move you."

"Okay, well, that's good. It hurts something awful though."

I knelt down and felt for a radial pulse on Abe's left wrist. "Does anything hurt besides your arm?"

"My back hurts quite a bit. Other than that, I'm not too bad."

"Can you feel me touch you?" I asked, gently touching different parts of Abe's left hand and fingers.

"Yes, I can feel it. That's good, right?"

"Yes, that's good. And you have a nice, strong pulse. Your left hand is quite cold, but of course, your right hand is very cold too because it's cold outside. We'll have to put a big dressing on your arm to try to keep the wood from moving on the trip to the hospital," I replied.

"Abe, I'm going to go get your wife," Fran interjected. "I don't think she realizes what's going on out here."

"Thanks. She has a bad cold, and she was taking a nap when I started. I guess she's probably sleeping through the whole thing. Thank God you heard me."

I reflected that Abe was truly blessed his neighbors heard his cries for help and came to his rescue. Soon it would be growing dark, and he could have been outside in the cold until his wife eventually woke up and realized he was missing.

Ted painstakingly put a cervical collar around Abe's neck, while Dillon and I placed a large, bulky dressing around his left arm. With help from Officer McGovern, we maneuvered him onto a backboard. By the time we got him loaded into the ambulance, his wife, Mabel, was ready to ride with us to the hospital.

Soon, we were giving our report to the triage nurse. Then, just like that, we were heading back home. We found out a few weeks later from Dwight and Fran Hawkins that Abe underwent arm surgery that very day and was on his way to making a full recovery. Although he had been quite literally on the fence, we received a call about six months later for a man who was on the fence figuratively.

. . . .

Diego Whittaker's stomach growled, pleading for a lunch break. Glancing at his wristwatch, he realized his stomach would have to keep growling for a while. Working on scaffolding more than 20 feet high was not exactly conducive to taking breaks or snacking.

Diego's partner, Hal Bronson, let out a loud sigh. "Hey, man, I'm hungry. How much longer until break time?"

"At least forty-five minutes," Diego replied, shrugging. He took off his baseball cap and wiped sweat from his forehead, enjoying the cool breeze on his damp head. He'd been in construction for the past 12 years. Heights never bothered him, and he actually enjoyed them most of the time. Since he was so experienced at his job, his boss often paired him with new employees. His partner, Hal, had been with the company for one week, though he'd bounced around numerous other construction companies. As far as Diego could tell, Hal didn't share his enthusiasm for the job.

"Man, why don't we go down early? I'm hungry and thirsty," Hal suggested, waving his arms in the air for emphasis.

"Easy there, you're rocking the scaffold," Diego said with concern, grabbing onto one of the ropes. Hal, unfazed, continued lamenting about wanting to take a break.

Diego heard an odd cracking noise. In shocked disbelief, he realized that the scaffolding was giving way. He watched in horror as Hal tried too late to grab onto a rope and instead tumbled backward off the scaffold. The remnants of the broken scaffold rocked violently in response, and Diego's grip on the rope was torn loose as he was thrown down hard. He felt himself skidding off what was left of the platform and managed to grab onto the rope once more with his left hand.

As he dangled from the platform, he asked, "Hal, are you okay? Can you get help?" Silence greeted his question. He managed a quick glance downward and then wished he hadn't. Hal lay unmoving and unresponsive on the ground directly below him.

"Help!" Diego shouted. Swinging his torso, he maneuvered himself and grabbed onto the rope with his right hand as well. Beads of sweat popped out on his forehead from the sheer effort of holding up his body weight. Unable to maintain his grip on the rope any longer, he closed his eyes and let go.

. . . .

DISPATCHER: "Request for first aid at 5 Chestnut Street for two men who have fallen at least twenty feet."

"I recognize that address. I think that house is under construction," Meg Potter said, climbing into one of the ambulances.

"Yes, they've been working on that home for a few months now," Ted replied. "I think there was a lull for a while though, when they weren't doing much of anything."

"Well, it definitely sounds like they're working on it now," Dillon said. "I'll grab this rig with Colleen and Andrea. Why don't you two roll the other one?"

Following Dillon's instructions, we climbed into our respective ambulances and drove the short distance to Chestnut Street. We pulled up in front of a large, partially built Colonial with a dark-blue dumpster parked in the driveway.

"There are two victims," Officer McGovern said by way of greeting as we jumped out of the rigs. "Hal Bronson, age 22, and Diego Whittaker, age 31. Hal is coming around now, but he was unconscious for at least two minutes. He's complaining of head and neck pain. It looks like he may have lost a few teeth. Diego landed feet first and didn't lose consciousness. He's complaining of foot and back pain."

"Are they around back?" I asked, swinging our large first aid bag over my shoulder.

"Yes, follow me," Officer McGovern replied.

As we rounded the back corner of the house, I spotted two men lying flat on their backs in a patch of mud. The graceful branches of a century-old oak tree shaded them from the sun. From the sounds of their moaning, it was easy to see that both men appeared to be in a great deal of pain.

Dillon, Colleen, and I went to assess Diego, while Ted and Meg assisted Hal. Diego's dark curly hair was soaked with sweat, and his beard had streaks of mud in it. His red flannel shirt, ripped from the fall, exposed numerous abrasions on his arms and torso.

"I'm not sure what happened," he told us. "One minute, I was thinking about my lunch break. The next minute, the scaffolding gave out, and Hal went crashing down. I was able to hold on for a couple minutes, but eventually I had to let go. I landed on my feet but then fell back onto my butt and hands."

Colleen performed a head-to-toe assessment, noting the obvious deformity of both of Diego's ankles. It looked like they may have both fractured upon impact with the ground. His low back was tender to the touch, but other than that, he looked remarkably good, considering what had happened.

Diego's blood pressure, pulse, and respiratory rate were all normal, so when paramedics Rose Anderson and William Moore arrived, Dillon quickly sent them over to Hal instead. Meanwhile, our team carefully applied a cervical collar, leg splints, and backboard to Diego.

"I really need my job. This is terrible. I'll probably be out of work for months," Diego said.

I patted him gently on the shoulder. I could have said something like, "Well, at least you're alive, and your bones will heal in time." But honestly, I don't think that's what he wanted to hear at that moment. Maybe later. For now, he simply needed to come to terms with his injuries. I knew he'd eventually recover and be able to return to work. But at this moment, undergoing possible foot and ankle surgery followed by several months of rehabilitation would probably seem like an eternity to him.

"You know, the funny thing is that lately I've been starting to think that I'm getting too old for this job. I've been on the fence about going back to school. I've been thinking about taking some classes and starting all over," Diego said.

"Well, you know, this might be a good time for you to take some online classes. See what else you might like to do with your life," I replied.

"Thanks. Maybe this is my wake-up call."

I glanced over at Hal. Rose was looking in his mouth with a penlight, probably counting how many teeth were missing. Meg was digging in the dirt with her fingers and suddenly waved something in the air. "I found two of the teeth!" I heard her exclaim. I wasn't sure if a dentist would be able to reattach the teeth or not, but at least he or she could take a look at them.

Neither of these men will be returning to their construction jobs in the near future, but they are incredibly blessed to be alive and talking to us right now. We never know what each day has in store for us. Since Diego mentioned he's on the fence about going back to school, I hope he takes this opportunity to explore finding a career that he enjoys and which will give him fulfillment.

. . . .

About that day or hour no one knows, not even the angels in heaven, nor the Son, but only the Father.

MATTHEW 24:36

Only God knows when it is time for us to join him in heaven. Abe, Diego, and Hal were truly blessed to survive their accidents.

9

Crash!

I waited patiently for the LORD;
he turned to me and heard my cry.
He lifted me out of the slimy pit,
out of the mud and mire;
he set my feet on a rock
and gave me a firm place to stand.

PSALM 40:1-2

Exhausted from a long day behind the cash register, Trixie Quartermain trudged through the top level of the parking garage toward her powder blue sedan. She had traded in her old SUV for the smaller car last summer to save gas money. The late afternoon sunrays momentarily blinded her. Shielding her eyes with one hand, she dug into her purse for her keys with the other.

Trixie plopped down onto the front seat of her car and closed her eyes for a minute. Sales had been very brisk in the jewelry department, and she'd scarcely had more than a minute or two to sit down all day. She felt a twinge of discomfort in the center of her chest but quickly brushed it aside. She'd been having brief episodes of chest and jaw pain for the past week. She wasn't a big fan of doctors and hospitals, but she finally relented and let her husband, Reggie, make an appointment for her to meet with a cardiologist later in the week. *Probably just indigestion, but I suppose it's better to get it checked out. A few tests will give us peace of mind.*

Shifting into gear, she began her trip home. The first 15 minutes passed uneventfully as she sang along with the car radio and contemplated what to make for dinner. Suddenly, however, a sharp stab of chest pain took her breath away. Trying to stay calm, she flipped on her right turn signal and began easing her car toward the shoulder.

Just as she was about to move her foot from the accelerator to the brake, she began to experience an odd floating sensation. Her head fell forward onto her chest as she lost consciousness. Her foot pushed down hard on the accelerator, and her car raced forward. Narrowly missing a parked vehicle, the sedan continued heading along its ill-fated course. As Bartholomew Road curved to the left, Trixie's car continued straight ahead, aimed directly at a century-old oak tree.

· · · · · · · · · · · · · ·

Lisa Cooper squeezed the nozzle of her garden hose, gently spraying water across her newly planted azalea bushes. She thought they were the perfect complement to her rhododendrons and yews.

She was jolted from her thoughts by the sound of a revving engine. Looking up from her bushes, she glanced back toward the road. She dropped the hose, watching in shocked disbelief as a car sped in her direction. Transfixed with horror, she watched as the car raced closer and closer toward the large oak tree that graced her property.

The sound of the impact briefly took her breath away, and she stifled a scream. She wanted to rush over to see if the person inside the car was okay, but her legs felt like rubber. After a second, her legs caught up with her brain, and she hurried toward the car.

Through the front windshield, Lisa could make out the figure of a middle-aged woman with brownish-gray hair slumped over the steering wheel. She yanked on the driver's side door, but she couldn't budge it. She wasn't sure if the car door was locked or simply too damaged from the accident to open. She rushed over to the passenger side door, but she couldn't open that either. With trembling fingers, she reached into her pocket, pulled out her cell phone, and dialed the local police department.

"Pine Cove Police. This is Dispatcher Franklin. How can I help you?"

"This is Lisa Cooper from Bartholomew Road. There's been a terrible accident in front of my house. Please send help right away. I can't get the doors open, and the woman's unconscious."

"How many cars are involved? Can you tell how many people are injured?" he asked.

"Just one car with a woman inside," Lisa replied. Her hands began trembling, and she gripped her phone more tightly.

"I'm going to dispatch the police, first aid, and fire department immediately. Please stay on the line," Dispatcher Franklin instructed.

. . . .

DISPATCHER: "Request for first aid and fire department in front of 221 Bartholomew Road for a motor vehicle accident with entrapment. Patient is unconscious at this time."

"We've got enough to roll two rigs. Let's go," Helen McGuire said. Ted O'Malley and I jumped in with her, while Archie Harris and Jose Sanchez hopped into a second ambulance. Jose had relocated to our town after retiring from a long career in politics. He began volunteering as an emergency medical technician because he felt a desire to give back to the community.

Helen parked the ambulance a bit down the street from the accident, leaving room for the fire truck to get close enough to utilize its extrication equipment. My eyes widened at the severe nature of the wreck. The front end of a small light-blue car was crushed against the trunk of an enormous, unforgiving oak tree. We each grabbed as much equipment as we could carry and hurried toward the car.

Sergeant Flint took a few steps in our direction. "I can't get the front doors open, but I managed to get one rear door partially open. She'll need to be extricated. I ran the license plates. The car comes back to a Trixie Quartermain. Dispatcher Franklin is trying to get hold of her family right now."

I glanced through the window and suppressed a shudder. Trixie's head had rolled forward onto her chest, her shoulder-length hair obscuring my view of her face. She remained completely motionless, with only the seat belt to keep her from completely falling over. I knew it was crucial that we get into the car as quickly as possible.

As if reading my thoughts, Fire Chief Watson said, "Why don't you squeeze one of your members into the back? Then we'll cut off the door—and the roof, too, if necessary."

Helen looked at me and nodded. Without any words, I knew what she wanted me to do. Since I was the smallest member, she wanted me to squeeze into the cramped rear quarters of the car. So I approached the car and slid through the narrow opening into the back.

I tapped Trixie's shoulder. *No response. Well, I didn't really expect one.* Helen passed a high-flow oxygen mask to me, and I carefully strapped it around Trixie's head as best as I could without moving her. Ted passed me two blankets, and I spread one over Trixie and one over myself. The blankets would help protect us from injury while the firefighters cut off the doors.

Now in a world of darkness, I groped with my hands until I found the sides of Trixie's head. I gently pulled it up off her chest to open her airway and allow her to breathe better. Also, in case she suddenly awakened, I wanted to make sure my hands were on her so she couldn't inadvertently be injured by the extrication tools.

"We'll talk you through the whole thing. We're starting now," Chief Watson said.

I closed my eyes and listened to the whirring noise of the tool as it began to grind through the metal. "We're going to get you out of here in a jiffy," I said to Trixie, even though I didn't think she could hear me. Even if she was aware of her surroundings, I doubted she could hear me over the noise of the power tools. But it made me feel better to say the words out loud anyway.

"How are you doing in there?" Chief Watson asked during a brief lull in the noise. "We're just about done."

"She's still unconscious." Trixie's breathing sounded shallow and labored. I hoped the paramedics were close by.

I heard the metallic crunching noise of the car door being peeled back, and before I knew it, Helen was helping me remove the blankets. "We'll do a rapid takedown," she said. "I'm putting a cervical collar on Trixie right now, and then we'll slide her onto the backboard."

Glancing out the window, I could see that the stretcher was perpendicular to the driver's side of the car, with a backboard balanced on top.

Helen slid the edge of the backboard underneath Trixie. "Just help the best you can from where you are," she instructed me.

I kept my hold on Trixie's head to keep her neck stable, and our team maneuvered her smoothly out of the car and onto the backboard and stretcher. While Jose and Archie strapped Trixie onto the backboard, I wiggled out of the rear of the car. *Okay, the hardest part is over. At least she's out. But is she going to be okay?*

Helen folded up the blanket. "We just got word from Trixie's husband. He's going to meet us at the hospital. He said she has an appointment in a few days with a cardiologist because she's been having chest pain on and off for the past week. So she may have had some sort of cardiac event that caused the accident."

I brushed some tiny glass fragments that had somehow found their way around the blanket off my pants. "That makes sense. She may have passed out before she even hit the tree."

Now that we were out of the car, I was able to take a closer look at Trixie. Although she was unconscious, her eyes were half-open. Their dark brown color stood in contrast to the marked pallor of her face.

"Her pulse is weak. Let's load her in the rig. I can see the medics pulling up now," Ted said.

I noticed that Trixie's breathing hadn't improved much even with high-flow oxygen. "Her respiratory effort is poor. We may have to start assisting with the bag valve mask."

"I'll run ahead and set up the bag valve mask in the rig," Archie said. The rest of us each grabbed a corner of the stretcher and quickly rolled it down a short length of pavement to the ambulance.

Paramedics Ty Fleming and Paula Pritchard began setting up their equipment in the back of the ambulance as we lifted Trixie inside. Helen gave them the patient report while I placed a mask over Trixie's nose and mouth. I coordinated squeezing the bag valve mask with her breathing efforts as best as I could.

Paula placed 12 electrodes various places on Trixie's chest, arms, and legs. "Let's get this heart monitor hooked up."

Meanwhile, Helen took Trixie's blood pressure. "It's low—96 over 56."

Ty drew blood samples and established an IV line.

Paula nodded toward the ECG screen. "Take a look at this."

"Seems to be a STEMI," Ty said. "I'll call in to medical control."

STEMI stands for ST-elevation myocardial infarction, a dangerous type of heart attack involving a blockage of one of the main coronary arteries. Trixie would have to be rushed into the cardiac catheterization lab right away. But the trauma team would need to make sure she was stable enough first.

"She's unresponsive, and her breathing is still very poor. I'm going to intubate her." Unzipping her airway kit, Paula assembled the necessary tools to stabilize Trixie's airway.

Ty pulled the keys to the medics' ambulance out of his pocket. "Do you have a driver for our rig? That way, we can both stay back here."

Jose nodded, grabbed the keys, and slipped out the rear doors of the ambulance.

Within a few minutes, we arrived at Bakersville Hospital. The trauma team met us at the door and ushered us into their suite. As we rushed by, I caught a glimpse of a middle-aged gentleman who looked as though he might collapse from shock. *That must be Trixie's husband.* One of the hospital's staff members took him by the arm and led him to a private room where he could sit and wait.

Judging by the sight of her car, Trixie was bound to have orthopedic and internal injuries, as well as possible head trauma. All these would only complicate her treatment for the heart attack. I knew she was in a very precarious state, and her chances for survival were uncertain at best.

Lord, please be with Trixie and her husband.

. . . .

My God sent his angel, and he shut the mouths of the lions. They have not hurt me, because I was found innocent in his sight. Nor have I ever done any wrong before you, Your Majesty.

DANIEL 6:22

Daniel tells us that God may send His angels to rescue us from danger. Our squad learned that on the night of the accident, Trixie underwent an emergency cardiac catheterization and received a stent to address the blockage in one of her coronary arteries. Two days later, when she was stable, she had a right pelvic fracture surgically repaired. She was also diagnosed with a severe concussion and multiple rib fractures. God blessed her by having the car crash witnessed by someone who was able to get her immediate help. I felt fortunate to be part of a team of volunteers, police officers, firefighters, and hospital staff who worked together to ensure that she could enjoy more years on earth.

10

Rough Start in Life

Be pleased to save me, Lord;
come quickly, Lord, to help me.

PSALM 40:13

Braxton-Hicks *contraction or premature labor?* Beth Alexander wasn't sure, but her level of concern rose exponentially each time her abdomen tightened. These didn't feel like the contractions she'd experienced in the past. They felt stronger, sharper, and some other indefinable quality that made them infinitely more frightening.

Beth and her husband, Jerry, had been trying to conceive for two years. When they had received the wonderful news six months ago from her obstetrician that she was six weeks along, she and Jerry had been ecstatic. Beth had been on cloud nine ever since, but there had been bumps along the way. Phrases like "incompetent cervix" and "gestational diabetes" flashed through her mind. Last night, she thought she might have seen a few small drops of blood in her underwear, but she'd brushed it aside. Now, the icy fingers of fear slid down her neck. *Maybe that really was blood. What if I'm miscarrying? What should I do? I wish Jerry wasn't at work.*

With trembling fingers, Beth picked up the phone and called her doctor's office. She wasn't surprised when her physician told her to go to the emergency room immediately. She had expected as much, and yet she still had found herself hoping that her doctor might say,

"Don't worry. Everything's fine. I'll see you at your regular appointment next week." After speaking with her doctor and calling Jerry, Beth quickly packed an overnight bag just in case she was admitted to the hospital. Then, taking a deep breath, she picked up her phone and dialed 911.

. . . .

DISPATCHER: "Request for first aid at 313 Horizon Avenue for a maternity call. Patient needs transportation to the hospital."

"I think we can roll with just the three of us," Darren Williams said to Ted O'Malley and me. Then he informed the dispatcher, "Dispatch, we're responding to Horizon Avenue." Two minutes later, we pulled up in front of a brown split-level home with green shutters.

We found Beth Alexander sitting on a chair close to the front door. A suitcase stood next to her. Her shoulder-length blond hair was pulled back in a braid, revealing her tear-stained face. "I'm sorry to trouble you. My husband's workplace is far away, and I definitely don't feel up to driving myself right now. My doctor said I need to go to the emergency room."

"That's what we're here for," I said. "I'm just going to check your pulse and blood pressure while Darren asks you a few questions."

"Okay, please do whatever you need to do. I'm seven and a half months pregnant. I've been diagnosed with an incompetent cervix and gestational diabetes. Other than that, I don't have any medical problems. I'm just praying my baby is okay. I think I might have bled a little last night. I'm terrified I might be miscarrying."

The ride to the hospital was mostly quiet. Beth was deep in thought, obviously worrying about what the doctor was going to find. After giving our patient report to veteran triage nurse Maggie Summers, we hugged Beth goodbye and wished her all the best.

. . . .

Several months later

Beth Alexander sat bolt upright in her bed. *Something's not right.* She tucked a strand of hair behind her ear and listened closely. *Peyton. It's Peyton. His breathing sounds funny.* Part of her wanted to jump out of bed to check on her son, and the other part of her was almost too petrified to move.

She tapped Jerry's shoulder. "Are you asleep?"

"I was," he replied groggily.

"I think something's the matter with Peyton."

Jerry rolled over and switched on the small lamp on his night table. "What's wrong?"

She quickly crossed the room to his crib. "I'm not sure, but doesn't he sound funny?"

"It's so dark in here. Let me turn on a brighter light," Jerry said. As he flipped the switch, they both gasped in dismay. Baby Peyton lay quietly in his crib, his breathing labored, his face blue.

Beth lifted Peyton into her arms. "What's wrong with him?" Her fears mushroomed into an all-too-frightening reality. *Not again, Lord. I almost lost him once already.*

"Remember, the cardiologist said this might happen," Jerry said, grabbing the cordless phone off the dresser and dialing 911. "We need an ambulance at 313 Horizon Avenue right away," he said into the phone. "Our baby's having trouble breathing, and he's turning blue!"

. . . .

DISPATCHER: "Expedite to 313 Horizon Avenue for an infant with severe difficulty breathing."

Ted slid behind the steering wheel. "Didn't we go to this house a while back for the woman with premature contractions?"

I climbed into the back of the ambulance to prepare the pediatric equipment. "Yes, I'm sure it's the same one. The good news is that she must not have miscarried."

Darren sat down next to me. "But it sounds like the baby's in trouble. I wonder if she gave birth right after we had the call for her."

"Quite possible, I suppose. She was already pretty far along," I said.

A minute later, we arrived at the familiar split-level home. The moon disappeared behind a cloud, so we had to rely on a lone streetlight to find our way. We hurried along the brick pathway and rushed through the front door, which someone had thoughtfully propped open for us.

"We're up here," Sergeant Flint called. We followed his voice to the small nursery on the second floor, where we found him holding a tiny baby in his arms. The infant's small face had an unnatural bluish hue, and his respirations were rapid and shallow. "I'm giving him oxygen, but I don't think it's helped much yet."

If Beth had looked worried the first time we had seen her, this time she was absolutely distraught. Her husband didn't look like he was faring much better. His skin was so pasty white that he looked as though he might pass out.

Tears streamed down Beth's face. "Please, do something," she pleaded.

On certain calls, we don't spend much time in the house assessing, but rather load the patient into the ambulance first and assess on the way. I knew we needed to move Peyton quickly into the rig. Ted and Darren were on the same wavelength. Darren scooped him out of Sergeant Flint's arms and headed downstairs. Ted trailed closely behind with the oxygen tank.

I bent to pick up the rest of our equipment. "What's been happening since we last saw you?"

"I had Peyton two days after you took me to the hospital. He was in the neonatal intensive care unit for a month. After he was born, we found out he has a PDA."

I glanced at Beth questioningly. "Do you mean a patent ductus arteriosus?" All babies are born with a ductus arteriosus, a vessel which allows blood to bypass the lungs and instead flow straight from the pulmonary artery to the aorta. It usually closes within a few hours of birth. Sometimes, especially with premature babies, it doesn't close on its own. This causes the lungs to fill with fluid, making it difficult for the infant to breathe.

"Exactly. And now, as a result, he has congestive heart failure," Jerry said.

"His cardiologist is trying to treat it with medications until he grows bigger. They'd like him to be six months old before they do surgery," Beth said.

Congestive heart failure. Heart surgery. Peyton's entry into the world had been difficult, and it appeared as if life hadn't gotten much easier since then.

"Please follow me to the ambulance," I said. "One of you can ride in the back with us, and one in the front. The paramedics from the hospital will be meeting us here in a minute."

"Thanks," Beth said. "The sooner we get there, the better. Peyton went down for the night okay, but then I woke up and thought his breathing sounded off. We called 911 right away. He seems like he's getting worse by the minute."

I led Jerry to the front seat and then helped Beth into the back of the ambulance. Medic team Arthur Williamson and Kennisha Smythe were already busy performing an assessment on Peyton. "If everyone's in, you can start rolling," Kennisha called up to Ted.

"I can drive your rig," I volunteered. Arthur tossed me the keys. We all recognized the urgency of the situation.

Flipping on the red flashing lights of the medics' rig, I followed behind our ambulance as we made our way toward Bakersville Hospital. Through the rear windows of our rig, I could see Darren, Arthur, and Kennisha all busily caring for Peyton. I figured that they were starting an IV line and providing lifesaving medications. *Please let him hold on until we get there.*

When we arrived at the emergency room, I jumped out of the medics' truck and pulled open the back doors to our ambulance. Peyton looked much the same as when I last saw him: bluish and struggling to breathe. *But he's still alive.*

The pediatric team met us at the door and escorted us into a specialized area geared to treat children. Peyton was whisked to the hospital's stretcher, and many competent hands began working together to help him. I took one last look at the pinched, worried faces of Beth and Jerry Alexander. They had traveled such a tough road already, and it looked like their troubles weren't over yet.

. . . .

This is how the birth of Jesus the Messiah came about: His mother Mary was pledged to be married to Joseph, but before they came together, she was found to be pregnant through the Holy Spirit. Because Joseph her husband was faithful to the law, and yet did not want to expose her to public disgrace, he had in mind to divorce her quietly.

But after he had considered this, an angel of the Lord appeared to him in a dream and said, "Joseph son of David, do not be afraid to take Mary home as your wife, because what is conceived in her is from the Holy Spirit. She will give birth to a son, and you are to give him the name Jesus, because he will save his people from their sins."

MATTHEW 1:18-21

Although the miracle of birth is a beautiful celebration of life, Peyton had a difficult start within the womb and after delivery. The Bible shows us that angels serve as ministers of the children of God. Peyton had heart surgery a week after we transported him to the hospital, and he made a full recovery.

11

Getting Back to Work

Let your face shine on your servant;
save me in your unfailing love.

PSALM 31:16

Lucas Rosewood had been working in the kitchen at the Pennington Manor for more than 35 years and had rarely missed a day of work. He loved the satisfaction he felt in preparing dishes for others to enjoy: creamy fettuccine Alfredo, succulent chicken française, mouthwatering chef salads, and tantalizing homemade soups and stews, to name a few.

Lately, however, his feet had really been bothering him. His podiatrist had said that he had plantar fasciitis and gave him injections in his feet. He had also said if that didn't help, he would fit him with orthotics and send him to physical therapy.

"Hey, Lucas, I need another steak. Medium rare, please," Lucinda, one of the waitresses, called across the kitchen.

"No problem," Lucas said. "For you, anything."

Lucinda had worked by his side in the restaurant for more than ten years. "Lucas, we're growing old together," she often said, and he would reply, "Not older, but better."

Lucas busied himself preparing the steak, while at the same time working on some other dishes. He enjoyed multitasking and loved staying busy. Since it was a weekend, tonight was exceptionally hectic.

He finished preparing a penne alla vodka dish and then gingerly strode across the kitchen to place the food in the area where a waitress would pick it up.

As he made his way back to his workstation, his foot suddenly slid on a wet spot. He tried to catch himself and grab onto the edge of a nearby counter, but it was just out of reach. Almost before he knew what was happening, Lucas was on the ground, the back of his head thumping hard on the tile floor. After lying stunned for a few seconds, he began silently berating himself.

Lucinda reentered the kitchen just in time to see Lucas fall. She rushed over and gave him a hand as he struggled to his feet. "Are you okay? Should I call for an ambulance? Maybe you should go to the hospital and get checked out."

Lucas politely shook off Lucinda's suggestion. "No, it's okay. Only my pride is hurt. I really need to finish preparing some of these other dishes."

The next hour passed in a blur of activity, and Lucas was so busy that he forgot all about his fall. He tried to keep up with the pace, churning out dishes as quickly as the orders piled in. But then, without warning, he began experiencing the worst, most crushing headache of his entire life. He grabbed onto the counter and looked around for a chair. Legs shaking, he held onto the edge of the counter as he worked his way over to a small metal stool.

Lucinda was in the kitchen at the time and noticed that Lucas sat down rather ungracefully. "You look terrible. What's wrong? Do you need some water?"

He shook his head. Lucinda's voice sounded far away, like she was speaking through a tank of water. "My head hurts so bad..." He closed his eyes and slid off the stool onto the floor.

"Lucas, what's wrong?" Lucinda quickly knelt next to him, gently shaking his shoulder. But Lucas, now unconscious, did not respond. "Someone, call 911. Lucas needs help!" She took off her apron, folded it into a small square, and placed it carefully under her friend's head. "Please, wake up."

• • • • • • • • • • • •

DISPATCHER: "Request for first aid at the Pennington Manor for a 64-year-old fall victim, now unconscious."

I was familiar with the layout of the Pennington Manor kitchen. We'd responded to a call there several months ago when one of the workers cut her finger and needed stitches. Dillon Chapman parked the ambulance near the rear entry to the restaurant, and Meg Potter, Archie Harris, and I hustled with our equipment into the kitchen.

"This is Lucas Gonzalez," a woman said, rising to her feet and stepping back a few steps to give us room to work. "He fell an hour ago and hit his head pretty hard on the floor, but he said he was okay and went back to work. Then a few minutes ago, he complained of a really bad headache and passed out. He hasn't moved since. Do you think he's going to be okay?"

"We're going to take him to the hospital so the doctors can figure out what's going on," Meg explained.

As she knelt down to assess Lucas, I went back outside to get a cervical collar and backboard. Dillon met me halfway and gave me a hand. "He's out cold," I said. "It sounds as if it may be a head injury related to a fall earlier this evening."

Dillon pulled a backboard out of the rear side compartment of the ambulance. "It could be some sort of brain bleed."

I grabbed a bag of cervical collars, and we reentered the kitchen. I knew head injuries that cause a sudden loss of consciousness could be extremely dangerous.

Meg tightened the strap on Lucas's oxygen mask. "He's got a large bump on the back of his head. It must have been quite a fall."

Officer Endicott, also on the scene, said, "We've got a two-minute ETA on the medics."

As we carefully placed a cervical collar around Lucas's neck and rolled him onto a backboard, he moaned softly but remained otherwise unresponsive. We lifted the backboard onto a stretcher and weaved around numerous stainless-steel counters to the exit. A light rain had begun falling, making the pavement slick. When we opened the rear ambulance doors to lift Lucas in, we found paramedics Ty Fleming and Paula Pritchard already setting up. "Officer Endicott told us what's going on. Let's take a look," Paula said.

I switched the portable oxygen tank to our on-board unit. "So far, he's been unresponsive."

"His pupils are slow to react to light." Paula shined a small penlight in Lucas's eyes. "Did he have any complaints before he went out?"

"Yes, he told his coworker that he had a terrible headache. Then he slid out of the chair onto the floor," Meg said.

Ty taped down the IV line. "It sounds like it could be a subarachnoid hemorrhage." A subarachnoid hemorrhage (SAH) would mean that Lucas was bleeding into his subarachnoid space, the fluid-filled area between the thin tissues that surround the brain.

Paula nodded her head in agreement. "He could be bleeding between the arachnoid and pia mater. I'll call ahead to trauma. Regardless, he'll need a CT scan stat."

"Don't people who have those kinds of bleeds have a poor prognosis?" Dillon asked.

"I'll say. There's a forty percent mortality rate. Let's hope we're wrong on this one, for Lucas's sake," Ty said.

Forty percent mortality rate. How often does each of us go to work, never thinking that we might have some awful sort of accident? That we might never be ourselves again. That we might never get to go home and see our family again.

When we arrived at the emergency room, we brought Lucas straight into one of the trauma bays. He remained completely unresponsive, his life hanging in the balance. I backed out of the room, comforted by the flurry of activity that surrounded Lucas. I knew that he would receive the very best care available.

. . . .

A few days later, our squad was dispatched to assist an elderly woman with chest pains. I was glad to see that Ty and Paula were the paramedics on duty. "Any word?" I asked eagerly. I didn't have to say anything else. They knew exactly whom I was asking about.

"Subarachnoid hemorrhage, just as we feared. He went for emergency surgery," Ty said.

"And?" I prompted, holding my breath as I awaited his answer.

"He's in the ICU, holding his own. We visited him yesterday. He's certainly not out of the woods, and he's not responding much yet, but he's definitely showing some signs of improvement," Paula said.

It wasn't the miraculous recovery I was hoping for, but it was a good start. I prayed that with time, Lucas would recover.

. . . .

Six months later

> **DISPATCHER:** "Request for first aid at the Pennington Manor, in the kitchen, for a severe nosebleed."

Alec Waters, Meg, and I were cleaning up the ambulance from the last call, so we drove immediately to the scene. As we stepped in the back door to the kitchen area, I tapped a gentleman on the shoulder and said, "We have a first aid call here. Do you know where our patient is?"

The man abruptly turned around, and I stopped dead in my tracks. "Are you…?"

"The man who fell and hit his head here six months ago?" he asked, finishing my question. "Yes, that's me. I'm back to work!"

"Oh, I'm so glad you're okay," I said, automatically giving him a big hug. Lucas hugged me back, a tight squeeze which almost took my breath away. *This is one of those unbelievable moments that make volunteering with the rescue squad so worthwhile.*

. . . .

During the night an angel of the Lord opened the doors of the jail and brought them out. "Go, stand in the temple courts," he said, "and tell the people all about this new life."

ACTS 5:19-20

In this verse, we see once again that angels may act as strengtheners and encouragers. An angel of the Lord encouraged the apostles to keep preaching after releasing them from prison. After his head injury, Lucas overcame dismal odds to recover and return to his job.

12

The Standby

Be strong and take heart,
all you who hope in the LORD.

PSALM 31:24

Tad Bayer was anxious to get home. For the fifth time in as many minutes, he glanced at the clock on his dashboard.

Tad pushed on, trying to ignore the pain in his stomach. Perspiration beaded his upper lip, and he impatiently swiped it away with the back of his hand. He cracked open the window, hoping that a little fresh air might lessen his nausea. He couldn't resist looking at the clock again. Only two minutes had passed since the last time he'd looked.

Tad had spent the day visiting his sister Ginger. They'd enjoyed going to a flower show in the morning and then a café for lunch. He'd had a delicious chef salad with garlic bread and a diet soda. *Could it have been something I ate? How quickly can you get food poisoning?* The highway seemed to stretch endlessly in front of him, and it started to seem like some of the lines on the road were getting fuzzy.

He edged his gray sedan off the highway and onto the shoulder. He turned off the engine and closed his eyes. After a few minutes of rest without feeling any better, he dug his cell phone out of his pocket and dialed home.

"Megan?" Tad asked when his wife picked up the phone.

"Yes, honey? Are you going to stay late with Ginger?" Tad heard Megan's hearing aid whistling as she turned up the volume, and the familiar noise comforted him.

"No, I'm already on my way home." Tad paused, drawing in a deep breath. "I pulled over because I don't feel good, and I'm not sure I can make it home." Now that he had verbalized his fear, it somehow made it seem that much more real and frightening.

"Where are you? I can try to find someone to come pick you up. I wish I could come get you myself." Because of her recent hip surgery, Megan wasn't cleared to drive yet.

"I don't want to trouble anyone." Tad cleared phlegm from his throat. "And I don't want you to worry." His wife had suffered a heart attack last year and ended up needing a stent for a blocked coronary artery. He didn't want to cause her any undue stress.

"Don't be silly. It's no trouble. This is what I'm going to do. I'm going to hang up and call the police to help find you. If you need an ambulance, they can call one for you."

"If you think that's for the best," Tad said, relieved that help would soon be on the way.

He heard rustling on the other end of the line and imagined that Megan had grabbed a pencil and paper. "Can you tell me where you are exactly? What are some landmarks?"

"I'm on Highway 101, but I'm not sure exactly where. I think I'm about an hour from home." He'd been feeling so crummy for the last half hour that he hadn't paid much attention to the scenery.

"Are there any signs near you? Something to help the police find you faster?"

"Not that I can see. I'm sorry about all this. I love you."

"Right back at you," she replied, a phrase that they had often said to each other over the decades. "Now, let me hang up so I can get some help, okay?" Silence greeted her. "Tad? Are you still there? Did you already hang up?"

. . . .

DISPATCHER: "Request for first aid to stand by at your building for a special assignment."

"What do you think it's for?" I asked as Alec Waters and Colleen Harper arrived at the first aid building.

"I'm not sure. I had my police scanner on, but I didn't hear any chatter," Alec said. "I'm going to call headquarters and see if they have an update for us." Before he could pick up the phone, our pagers went off again.

DISPATCHER: "Please stand by in front of 1621 Kingston Avenue and wait in your ambulance. An officer will come out to your rig and give further instructions."

"Sounds intriguing," Colleen commented, slipping behind the steering wheel.

"Maybe a crisis patient," I guessed. "Or a domestic dispute?" Occasionally, the dispatcher will instruct us to wait outside until the scene is safe for us to proceed.

After a short drive, we pulled up in front of a small Cape Cod–style house. Fog rolled down the road, making it difficult to see clearly. Officer Sims's head suddenly appeared close to the driver's side of the rig.

"What's up?" Colleen asked as she rolled down the window. I craned my head through the small opening between the rear section of the rig and the front cab so I could hear Officer Sims's reply.

"The call is actually for several doors down. We wanted to keep you guys well out of view. We've come to break the news to an elderly woman that her husband was found deceased in his car a short while ago."

I let out a gasp of dismay. "That's so horrible." *That poor woman. Her whole world is about to change with the ring of her doorbell.*

"This is one of those nights where I don't really like my job," Officer

Sims said. "We know the woman has a heart condition. We thought it would be a good idea to have you close by in case something goes wrong."

"We'll stay here as long as you need us. I just wish we could do more," Alec said. Officer Sims waved and disappeared into the fog.

After about 45 minutes, the dispatcher released us. My heart ached for a nameless, faceless woman who had just received such terribly sad news.

Dear Lord, please be with this woman tonight in her time of sorrow.

. . . .

Five years later

I knelt down and strapped two-pound cuff weights around my outpatient's ankles. "I'm going to try heavier weights today." Jeanette had recently undergone a total knee replacement, and we were working on increasing her strength and improving her gait during her physical therapy sessions. So far, she was making excellent progress. Instead of using a walker, she was now able to walk short distances with a cane.

"I just wish that Ernie were here to see how well I'm doing," she said wistfully, a faraway look in her eyes.

"Was that your husband's name?" I knew Jeanette was widowed, but I didn't know more than that.

"Yes, he was the light of my life. You know, it's only been three weeks." She turned her face away from me for a second. I was pretty sure she didn't want me to see the tear sliding down her cheek. Wordlessly, I handed her a tissue.

"I'm so sorry. I had no idea it was so recent. That must have been right around the time you had your surgery."

"Yes, I had been home only a few days when it happened. Ernie called me from the highway and said that he didn't feel well," Jeanette said. I patted her shoulder, waiting for her to continue. "By the time the police found him, he was already gone."

An odd feeling washed over me as I recalled the night five years before when we'd had the special standby assignment. "That's terrible.

I'm so sorry." I reached across one of the parallel bars to give Jeanette a hug.

She sighed. "If we could have just found him sooner. Maybe he would have had a chance."

The years suddenly melted away as I thought back to the night when I'd prayed for a nameless, faceless woman who had so tragically lost her husband. Now, suddenly, a woman with very similar circumstances stood before me. *Dear Lord, please be with Jeanette as she works through her grief. Please let her be consoled by the fact that she and Ernie will one day be reunited in Your kingdom.*

. . . .

An angel from heaven appeared to him and strengthened him.
LUKE 22:43

When Jesus prayed to His Father, God sent an angel to strengthen Him. Sometimes, it is the family members left behind, such as Megan and Jeanette, who need the strengthening and encouragement of angels.

13

Two Gentlemen

We are brought down to the dust;
our bodies cling to the ground.
Rise up and help us;
rescue us because of your unfailing love.

PSALM 44:25-26

Trevor Nolan blinked twice, the warm morning sun shining brightly into his eyes. Since he retired several years ago, he had a daily morning ritual: eating a breakfast of warm oatmeal with a banana and glass of orange juice, shaving, taking a steaming-hot shower, and then riding his bicycle to town to buy the daily newspaper. He knew he could have the paper delivered, but he preferred the exercise, as he wasn't getting any younger. And he wasn't a big fan of the online edition; he liked to read the paper in his sunroom and not be tied down to his office computer.

After completing the first parts of his routine, Trevor started his trip to town. He slowed his bike and stopped briefly at a three-way intersection before proceeding. Since he tended to leave his house at the same time every day, he often ran into the same people. He waved to Delia Lane, who was puttering in her flower garden in her front yard. She paused and, switching her clippers to her left hand, waved to him with her right. "Morning," she called out.

Next, he passed a young man walking a Great Dane. He didn't

know the man's name, but they always exchanged greetings and quick pleasantries about the weather.

Seemingly out of nowhere, beads of cold sweat formed on Trevor's forehead and above his upper lip. Within a minute, he began feeling lightheaded. Concerned that he might pass out and fall, he slowly brought his bike to a halt and sat down on the curb. Grabbing his water bottle out of its holster, he shakily took a few sips. Several long minutes passed, but he didn't feel any better. *Should I ring someone's doorbell and ask for help? Or should I try to bike the rest of the way to town?*

Undecided, he remained perched on the edge of the curb. A minute later, a gray sport utility vehicle pulled up and parked close to him. With relief, Trevor recognized his longtime friend Bart Stuckey.

Bart climbed out of his vehicle and slowly shuffled toward him. "Trevor, is that you? What are you doing?" He pulled his cap farther down to shield his eyes from the sun and peered at his friend.

"I don't feel good. I'm not sure what's wrong, but I'm glad you stopped. I really wasn't sure what I was going to do."

"You're as white as a ghost. Stay right there. My phone's in my car. I'm going to call for an ambulance." Bart shuffled back toward his car.

Trevor closed his eyes and fervently hoped that the ambulance would arrive quickly.

· · · · · · · · · · · · ·

DISPATCHER: "Request for first aid in front of 294 Hudson Avenue for an elderly man who is not feeling well."

Meg Potter and I scurried into the back of the ambulance, while Dillon Chapman hopped onto the driver's seat. He smoothly pulled the rig out into traffic. "We're responding," he notified the dispatcher.

"If you pass me the clipboard, I'll start writing down some info," Meg said.

After silently passing her the clipboard, I quickly donned a pair of medical gloves. Before I knew it, the ambulance was pulling up to the scene. A decidedly pale older gentleman wearing a navy polo shirt sat on the curb. A large sycamore tree's graceful branches were providing him with shade. Officer Endicott and another elderly gentleman wearing a navy-blue windbreaker stood next to him.

The pale gentleman leaned backward against the trunk of the tree. "I'm Trevor Nolan. Thanks for coming. I feel like I'm going to pass out."

His pulse ox level was only 89 percent (normal is 95 to 100 percent), so I placed a high-flow oxygen mask over his nose and mouth, cinching the green elastic strap tight to keep it in place. "We're going to lay you down on our stretcher, which should help you to feel a little better." I slid my fingers onto his wrist to check his pulse. "One hundred and weak, but regular," I said to Meg, who jotted the information down.

Meg, Dillon, Officer Endicott, and I gently lifted Trevor from the curb onto the stretcher.

"I just checked in with dispatch," Dillon said. "The medics are unavailable. Let's load him in the ambulance and head to the hospital. We can finish his assessment on the way."

Meg and I settled into the back of the ambulance. While I finished assessing Trevor, Meg asked him about his past medical history, medications, and allergies.

"I think the oxygen is helping. I'm starting to feel better." Trevor turned to me and raised one eyebrow inquiringly. "Hey, I know you. You're one of those beach cops."

The way he said it wasn't exactly a compliment, so I had a feeling he had more to say on the topic of special officers.

"Yes, that's my summer job," I replied. At the time, I was in college and spent the summers working at the beach.

Trevor tapped his fingers on the side rail of the stretcher. "Do you remember that morning in July when you told me to walk my bike?"

"I can't say that I do, but to be honest with you, we tell people to walk their bikes all the time. You can only ride them on the boardwalk before six o'clock in the morning in the summer."

Trevor scowled. "It's a dumb rule. Who makes up these rules?"

"I'm truly sorry, but I didn't make the rule. It's just my job to try to enforce it." I slid back on the rig's bench to give him a little more space.

"Yes, I know. I don't mean to grumble at you. I get it. You're just doing your job. But that doesn't make it any less annoying."

I tried to change the topic. "How long have you lived in Pine Cove?"

"Thirty-seven years. I love it here. It's a great place to raise a family," Trevor replied.

"Isn't that the truth. It's a wonderful place to live," Meg agreed.

"Hey, were you two there when my friends Madeline and Perry Parker almost died?" Trevor asked.

"I sure was," I replied. Shortly after the Parkers had returned home from grocery shopping, Madeline began feeling ill and fell unconscious. Perry also began feeling unwell, and with his last bit of strength he was able to call the police department and utter the words, "My wife…help." Officers Fred Smith and Jim Jones had broken down the front door and carried the Parkers next door to their neighbor's house. Our first aid squad had provided emergency first aid, including rescue breathing. It turned out that the Parkers had accidentally left their car running in the garage after they went shopping. Unbeknownst to them, their house had filled with deadly carbon monoxide fumes. Had it not been for the quick thinking of our dispatcher, the heroic actions of our police officers, and the grace of God, the Parkers would surely have died that night. Instead, they were blessed to enjoy many more happy years together.

"The police and your squad did a tremendous job," Trevor said. "You saved their lives. I just had dinner with them the other night, and they're both doing great."

I was extremely glad to hear it. I felt truly fortunate to have played a role in their survival. "We're pulling into the emergency room parking lot right now."

A few minutes later, we met veteran nurse Maggie Summers at the triage desk. Both organized and efficient, she kept the emergency department running as smoothly as a philharmonic orchestra in concert. Meg gave her our report, adding that the paramedics were not available.

Maggie pointed down the hallway. "You can put him in room 4."

As we rolled him from Maggie's desk to his new quarters, I couldn't help but notice how much better he looked now than he did a mere half hour ago. I shook his hand. "Feel better. I hope you're home soon and back to biking around town."

Dr. Parnell, an outstanding emergency physician, stepped into the room as I was stepping out. *Trevor's in great hands. I know he'll receive the best possible care.*

. . . .

Delia Lane liked routines. She appreciated the predictability of knowing exactly what each day had in store for her. She enjoyed spending some time each morning puttering in her garden, whether that meant pulling some weeds, watering plants, or inhaling the exquisite fragrance of one of God's most wonderful creations—flowers.

Earlier that morning, she'd waved absentmindedly at her friend Trevor Nolan as he bicycled past her home. Sometimes while she was gardening, he stopped to chat for a few minutes. Today, however, he seemed lost in thought, much the same way she was. Delia's husband, Sebastian, had said he wasn't feeling very well that morning when he got out of bed. "I feel like I'm coming down with something. I feel fatigued, like there's a strange heaviness all over my body," he'd told her.

She'd set up her husband at their kitchen table with decaf coffee, a banana, and two slices of warm, buttered toast. He assured her that he was fine and that perhaps the feeling would pass quickly. So, after trimming a few more branches from a gold dust plant, she decided to go back inside and check on him.

. . . .

Using a remote control, Sebastian flipped on the small, wall-mounted flat-screen television in his kitchen. He took a sip of coffee, relishing its rich flavor and aroma. Since it was cooling off, he decided to place it in the microwave for a few seconds. He started to rise to his feet, but his legs felt heavy, and he slowly sank back down into his chair. He wasn't usually one to worry, but he was starting to grow more concerned. When he glanced at the clock on the oven, the bright white numerals seemed oddly dark.

I hope Delia comes back inside soon. Sebastian and Delia first met in college about 50 years earlier. He liked to tell people that he swept her off her feet in chemistry class. The pair got married right after school and had been living in Pine Cove, Sebastian's hometown, ever since. They had raised three children together, and now they were enjoying spending time with their five grandchildren.

He glanced at the clock again. Sunbeams found their way through the wooden blinds, casting thin rays of light across the kitchen table. He had the strangest sensation that time was suddenly freezing and that this moment of discomfort could last an eternity. He wanted to cry out for help but couldn't speak. A strange wave of disquiet swept over him. He closed his eyes and let the tide sweep him away.

· · · · · · · · · · · · ·

"Sebastian? Are you feeling any better?" Delia asked as she rounded the corner from the foyer into the kitchen. She heard a strange noise, like a combination of a gasp and a moan. Almost immediately, her eyes were drawn to the floor on the far side of the kitchen table, between two chairs.

"Sebastian, wake up! Talk to me." Delia dropped to her knees on the ground next to him and touched his cheek.

He began shaking all over, his arms and legs growing rigid. He struggled for each breath. His blue lips appeared garish in his grayish-white face.

Scrambling to her feet, Delia rushed to the cordless phone on the kitchen counter. With trembling fingers, she dialed 911. "My husband needs help…"

· · · · · · · · · · · · ·

DISPATCHER: "Request for first aid at 102 Cherry Blossom Lane for a medical emergency."

Grabbing the mic with his right hand, Dillon said, "We're responding. Please have any available members meet us at the scene." We'd just finished dropping off Trevor Nolan at the hospital, so now we were only about a minute away from Cherry Blossom Lane.

"Received. As per patrols on scene, expedite. Patient is seizing," Dispatcher Franklin said.

As soon as we arrived at the scene, we rushed with our equipment along a short cobblestone walkway, through a spacious foyer, and into a bright, sunny kitchen. Large green spider plants hung from the ceiling in the far corner, adding an additional sense of warmth to the room. I could see two slim, blue plaid pajama–clad legs sticking out from behind the kitchen table.

"Sebastian wasn't feeling well this morning," an older woman with short, wavy brown hair said. "I'm his wife, Delia Lane. I was working in our garden and just came in to check on him. I found him on the floor and called 911 right away."

"He stopped seizing just a few seconds ago," Officer Endicott added. "I placed him on high-flow oxygen."

Meg placed a pulse oximeter on Sebastian's left index finger. "He's very cyanotic. Blood oxygen saturation is 83 percent. Respirations are only 8."

I knew such a low respiratory rate would not provide Sebastian with enough oxygen. We'd have to assist his breathing, so I pulled a bag valve mask from our jump kit.

"I'll finish getting the rest of his vital signs and see if he has a gag reflex," Meg said.

Dillon pulled Mrs. Lane aside, and I could hear him asking her questions about her husband's past medical history.

Mrs. Lane raked her fingers through her hair. "He's always been pretty healthy. He had gallstones about five years ago, and his prostate is enlarged. He doesn't take any medications, and he doesn't have any allergies that I know of."

"Medics are just two minutes out," Officer Endicott said, heading toward the front door. "I'll direct them in and let them know what's going on."

"Can you hand me an oral airway?" Meg asked. I measured one from the tip of Mr. Lane's ear to the corner of his mouth before silently handing it to her. She deftly inserted it to keep his tongue from obstructing his airway.

I was relieved when paramedics Rose Anderson and William Moore stepped into the kitchen. Although the oral airway helped keep Mr. Lane's airway patent, he really needed to be intubated.

Rose, formerly a medic in the Midwest, relocated to our area when she got married. William used to be an accountant but switched to the medical field a few years earlier when he got tired of number crunching. Working together seamlessly, the pair intubated Mr. Lane and established an IV line.

"His situation is precarious at best. We're going to need to put him on a backboard in case we need to start chest compressions," Rose said.

Dillon, Meg, and I rolled Mr. Lane onto a backboard, while Rose protected his airway and took over ventilations. Using a four-person lift, we carried him out to the sidewalk, where Officer Endicott had set up our stretcher. Within a minute, we were on our way to Bakersville Hospital.

I couldn't help but compare our first patient that morning, Trevor Nolan, with Sebastian Lane. Although Trevor hadn't been in the best shape, he certainly seemed to have fared better than Sebastian. I wasn't sure what was wrong with Sebastian, but Rose and William felt that his troubles stemmed from a life-threatening cardiac arrhythmia. His life now hung in the balance, the pull of heaven against the counterforce of earth. I wasn't sure which would win out. As a Christian, I knew I had to have faith that, whatever happened, it was ultimately part of God's plan.

When we arrived at the hospital, Rose heaved the heart monitor onto the small net on the back of the stretcher. "His blood pressure is bottoming out. Let's get him inside right away."

I helped Mrs. Lane out of the front seat of the ambulance. "Is he doing any better?" she asked.

I couldn't look directly into her eyes, since I wasn't prepared to witness the anguish I knew I would see there. Instead, I focused my gaze on her forehead, close to her hairline. "He's about the same," I replied, squeezing her hand.

"Room 3," Maggie said, directing us after Rose gave her the patient report. We moved a few doors down and transferred Sebastian from our stretcher to the hospital's gurney. A flurry of activity immediately surrounded him as Dr. Parnell, a respiratory therapist, and several nurses and technicians attended to his needs.

I glanced across the hall and noticed that the room into which we had brought Trevor Nolan a short time ago now stood empty. Stepping out into the hallway, I spotted Maggie at her desk. "Where's the gentleman whom we just brought in a half hour ago, Trevor Nolan?"

"He's, uh, well, he didn't make it," Maggie replied, shaking her head.

"I can't believe it!" I exclaimed. "He's gone? He died?"

"He coded about three minutes after you left. We defibrillated him immediately, but we never brought him back. I guess it was just his time." She patted my shoulder. "You guys did a great job."

Another squad was rolling in with a patient, so I stepped aside and tried to make sense of what Maggie had just told me. I knew that Sebastian Lane might not make it, but I had fully expected Trevor to survive. He'd just been speaking about the Parkers, who so miraculously survived the carbon monoxide poisoning. When we discussed them, it never occurred to me that Trevor himself could die so suddenly.

I learned several weeks later that Sebastian Lane made a full recovery and was home again with his wife. And so, the gentleman I thought would live never made it home, but the one I thought was in grave peril survived.

Live each day as though it could be your last, for you never truly know when the kingdom of the Lord is at hand.

. . . .

I am Gabriel. I stand in the presence of God, and I have been sent to speak to you and to tell you this good news.

LUKE 1:19

There are numerous examples in the Bible in which angels serve as messengers, such as the verse above from Luke in which the angel Gabriel tells Zechariah that his prayers had been answered and that his wife, Elizabeth, would have a son, who would be named John. Six months after Elizabeth became pregnant, Gabriel visited Mary and told her that she would conceive a son who would be named Jesus (Luke 1:26-33).

Sometimes, the messages we receive are good news, like when I learned Sebastian Lane returned home with his wife. Others, such as learning that Trevor had died, have the opposite effect. If we listen closely, we may hear the messages that Jesus might be sending us about our own lives as well as the lives of others.

14

Lost!

*Let all the faithful pray to you
while you may be found;
surely the rising of the mighty waters
will not reach them.
You are my hiding place;
you will protect me from trouble
and surround me with songs of deliverance.*

PSALM 32:6-7

ola Perez's eyes popped open. A small nightlight partially lit the room, and its warm glow caused the ceiling fan's shadows to dance merrily on the wall. *I can't lie here all day just looking at shadows. I need to get a move on. If I leave right now, I can get there on time.* She wasn't exactly sure where "there" was, but she knew she had to at least try to make it. She worried that maybe someone was counting on her. She didn't want to let them down.

Lola glanced over at her husband, Enrique, who was fast asleep under the warm plaid comforter. She noticed how his graying hair shone almost silver in the glow of the nightlight. *Best to let him sleep. He might not want me to try to get there right now.* Quietly, she slid on her terry robe and a pair of powder-blue fuzzy slippers. She padded softly across the hardwood floor, taking care not to make any noise. After closing the bedroom door behind her, she silently made her way down the stairs to the front door. Enrique had put an alarm on it, but she'd already figured out how to disarm it. After disengaging it, she slipped out into the darkness.

She found the cold stillness of the night both calming and invigorating at the same time. Lengthening her stride as much as her slippers would allow, she set out in earnest for her unknown destination. She didn't pay attention to the fact that the traffic light at the corner was red and headed across the street without hesitation.

The driver of a beige minivan honked and slammed on his brakes, just narrowly missing Lola. She didn't seem to notice and walked onward, almost as if in a trance. Her toe caught an uneven slab of slate on the sidewalk, and she briefly lost her balance. After regaining her footing, she forged ahead with renewed determination. Even though she didn't know where she was going, she was positive that she would know when she got there.

· · · · · · · · · · · · ·

Enrique Perez's alarm roused him from a deep sleep. Almost immediately, he sensed that something wasn't right. As he rolled over onto his left side, his eyes were automatically drawn to the other side of his queen-size bed.

His heart thumping wildly, Enrique jumped out of bed. "Lola!" he shouted urgently, the sound of his voice echoing in the hallway. He half walked, half ran from room to room, yelling her name as he went. But within just a matter of minutes, he was forced to accept the grim truth. She was gone. *Again.*

Grabbing his phone, Enrique punched in the all-too-familiar number of the Pine Cove Police Department. "I'd like to report a missing person," he began.

· · · · · · · · · · · · ·

The first rays of morning sunshine crept through the darkness, lighting the way for Lola. In the distance, a bright neon sign caught her attention. *"Midge's Diner—breakfast, lunch, and dinner."* That's it. *That's where I'm going.* Seemingly unaware of the numerous approaching cars, she jaywalked across the highway. She paused at the diner's front entrance, a bright smile lighting her face as she peered through the window. She eagerly pulled open the heavy aluminum door, and her stomach growled loudly as she caught a whiff of fresh-baked pastries, pancakes, maple syrup, and bacon.

A middle-aged woman wearing a light blue dress with a white frilly apron greeted her. "Hi, sweetie. I'm Midge. Can I help you?"

"Yes, some breakfast would be terrific. I'm looking forward to sitting down for a bit," Lola replied.

Midge eyed Lola's house robe and slippers and raised one eyebrow questioningly. "Long night?"

Lola nodded and followed Midge to a small booth toward the back of the diner.

"Let me start you off with something to drink. Coffee? Tea?"

Lola fidgeted with the buttons on her robe. "Coffee sounds wonderful. Thank you."

Midge returned a minute later with a mug and a carafe of coffee and poured a cup. "Cream? Sugar?" When Lola nodded, Midge added both to the coffee. Then she slid onto the booth's seat across from Lola. "Now, why don't you tell me where you're from."

"Oh, you know, here and there."

"Are you in some sort of trouble that you had to leave your house quickly?"

Lola smiled. "Oh no. No trouble. I just knew I had to go and then come here, you know?" She stopped fiddling with her robe buttons long enough to take a sip of coffee.

"Okay, then. What can I get you to eat?" Midge scribbled down Lola's order, then headed straight to the phone behind the serving counter. Quickly, she dialed the number of the local police department. "I was wondering if you have any reports of a missing elderly woman."

. . . .

Dillon Chapman, Ted O'Malley, and I arrived at the home before our patient did. Officer Endicott met us on the front porch. "We were here several times weeks ago. Lola Perez has Alzheimer's disease. Her husband, Enrique, has been trying his best to keep her at home. He really doesn't want her to go to a nursing home. But as you can see, it's been a struggle for him. If you want to come inside, you can ask him some questions before she gets home."

I removed my pen's cap and prepared to start writing the call sheet. "Where's she coming from?"

"Midge's Diner," Officer Endicott replied.

"Why, that's six miles away!" Ted exclaimed. "How'd she get so far?"

"We're trying to figure out if she walked the whole way or if she somehow caught a bus or got a ride or something."

We stepped inside a small two-story Colonial with an open floor plan. Lots of small potted plants lined the windows in the kitchen and the bay window in the living room, making the home seem warm and inviting. I walked across an Oriental rug, faded and worn from years of use, and headed through the living room into the kitchen.

Enrique sat at the kitchen table, his head in his hands. His arthritic fingers kept sliding nervously through his short salt-and-pepper hair, almost as if he was literally trying to pull it out from the roots. He glanced up at us as we entered the room but quickly slumped down again, his hands returning to his head. "What can I do? I don't know what to do. How can we go on like this?"

Ted, Dillon, and I slid into the empty chairs at the table. "It must be so difficult for you," I said. I figured that the strain of constantly trying to keep track of his wife must be wearing him down.

"You have no idea. I don't get any sleep. I can't turn my back for one second, or she's gone." He pushed his chair back as if to stand up but then changed his mind.

"How long has she been like this?" Dillon asked.

"We had forty-five wonderful years together. Then five years ago, Lola lost her short-term memory. She's been getting progressively worse, but the past two months have been absolutely terrible."

Officer Endicott jumped in. "We're going to call Social Services to come out and try to help you figure out a plan. Perhaps they'll have some suggestions."

Enrique stared morosely at a half-filled glass of orange juice. "Okay."

"How about adult day care?" I asked. I knew there was at least one such center near my workplace.

Enrique shifted his gaze from the glass of orange juice to me. "What's that? I've never heard of it."

I explained how people who require supervision can spend the day there, keeping busy with various activities and exercise classes.

"If Lola spent three hours a day in a place like that, I could get my errands and shopping done without worrying so much. Thank you. I'll check into it." The possible solution seemed to give him a ray of hope, and for that, I was grateful.

A moment later, Lola arrived home with a burly police officer from another town. She was all smiles, completely unaware that she had caused her husband so much worry. "Wow, there's a party going on here!" she exclaimed, noting all the unfamiliar faces in her kitchen.

"You scared me half to death running out like that," Enrique chided.

"Oh, I was out for a little walk is all," she replied, her smile fading briefly. "I met a really nice lady and this man." She pointed to the police officer. "He gave me a ride home. Wasn't that so kind of him?"

"Well, let's just check you out and make sure you're okay," Ted said as he led her to sit down at the kitchen table. He pulled a blood pressure cuff out of our first aid bag and proceeded to check her vital signs. "Everything appears to be normal."

We said our goodbyes, and soon we were on our way. Lola was fortunate that Midge took the time to make sure she returned safely home from the diner.

· · · · · · · · · · · · ·

*An angel of the Lord said to Philip, "Go south to the road—the
desert road—that goes down from Jerusalem to Gaza."*

ACTS 8:26

Sometimes, angels act as guides, pointing out the way. Some
families carry a difficult burden trying to care for loved ones
and need guidance. Dementia was slowly robbing Lola of her
memories and her ability to think clearly. I admired Enrique's
steadfast determination to do his best by his wife. I prayed that
Social Services would figure out how to provide him with some
much-needed relief.

15

Struggling to Breathe

Be merciful to me, LORD, for I am in distress;
my eyes grow weak with sorrow,
my soul and body with grief.

PSALM 31:9

Rod Blackwell threw open the back door to his home and plopped down onto a small wooden bench. "Mom, I need my inhaler!" Each breath took a tremendous amount of effort as he worked hard to force air into his lungs.

Shirley Blackwell came running toward her son with his inhaler in her hand. "I told you to always bring this with you when you go for a jog," she said with a mixture of exasperation and concern. "Your wheezing sounds terrible."

Rod shrugged as he reached for the inhaler. "I didn't have pockets. And I don't like to carry it in my hand."

"You're 15 years old now. You're old enough to know better. I may not always be here to help you. What if I'm at work? I'd feel a lot better if you'd start taking more responsibility." Shirley worked long hours in retail, and Rod was often on his own.

"Uh-oh," Rod said. "My inhaler's empty. I must not have noticed the last time I used it. Do we have another one in the medicine cabinet?" He leaned forward on the bench, placing his forearms on his thighs as he struggled to breathe.

"This is exactly what I'm talking about. You need to start managing your asthma better. You can't keep riding along on a wing and a prayer. I'll go look for your inhaler."

Shirley returned a minute later empty handed. "I can't go to the drugstore now. It'll take too long. I'll have to call for the medics."

"You better do it fast, Mom. I—really—can't—breathe," Rod wheezed.

. . . .

DISPATCHER: "Request for first aid at 382 Bergen Street for a medical emergency. Medics are responding from the hospital."

"Last time we went there, it was for a woman with diabetes," I mused as I climbed into the ambulance. "I think her name is Shirley. Maybe she's having another diabetic emergency."

"Yes, I was on that one too. She's been having a hard time controlling her sugar levels," Colleen Harper said.

"We've been there quite a few times. I wonder if she's a candidate for one of those insulin pumps," Helen McGuire remarked.

"Are you all sitting?" Archie Harris asked. He flipped on the lights and sirens, and we headed toward Bergen Street.

DISPATCHER: "Patient update: Fifteen-year-old male having an asthma attack."

"I guess I'm wrong; it's not for Shirley," I said. "I remember the last time we were there, she mentioned that she's a single mom. Maybe it's her son."

Archie backed onto the driveway by a small yellow cottage with bright blue shutters and trim. "You all go in," he said. "I'll follow with the stretcher." A Pine Cove Police car was already parked in front of the house, close to a basketball hoop.

Colleen knocked on the front door, and the three of us trooped through the living room toward the rear of the house. I could hear wheezing long before we found Officer McGovern, Shirley Blackwell, and a teenage boy in a small laundry room behind the kitchen. The boy's face was unnaturally white, and his hair was plastered to his scalp from perspiration.

"I'm so sorry," Shirley apologized. "Rod ran out of his medication. I think he'd be fine if he could just take some puffs of his inhaler." She looked at us more closely. "Oh, you're the girls who were here last time when it was for me. Thank you."

Officer McGovern adjusted the gauge on the oxygen tank. "I just put Rod on fifteen liters per minute, but I think he really needs a breathing treatment."

We got to work. "Pulse ox is 85 percent, and heart rate is 110. Let me check his blood pressure," Helen said. As she finished auscultating the blood pressure, paramedics Rose Anderson and William Moore entered the room.

"Well, young man, what's going on?" William greeted him.

"I shouldn't—have run—without my—inhaler. And—I—shouldn't have—let it—run out."

Rose quickly administered a nebulizer treatment.

Within a matter of minutes, Rod was feeling much better. "I don't have to go to the hospital. I'm fine now, everyone. Thanks for helping me."

Shirley promised she would be with Rod for the rest of the day and she'd call us back if he needed more help. "We're going to the pharmacy right now to pick up another inhaler."

· · · · · · · · · · · · · ·

Several months later

"Mom, I need my inhaler!" Rod shouted as he entered the house through the back door. He rushed into the kitchen and leaned on the counter as he struggled to get air into his lungs. "Mom!" The house was silent, except for the hum of the refrigerator. He glanced at the small antique clock on the wall. *She must still be at work.*

He struggled to his feet and made his way, step by step, to his bedroom. Grabbing his inhaler, he took several puffs. He had two different types of inhalers now, so he took several puffs of the second one as well. Feeling suddenly shaky, he sat down on the edge of his bed. *I hope they work fast. My chest feels so tight.*

A few minutes passed, but Rod's chest continued to feel tight, and he remained short of breath. Unsure of what to do, he called his mother at her workplace.

"Rod, is that you? What's wrong? Is it your breathing again?" Shirley asked with alarm.

"Yeah. The inhalers—aren't working. I can't breathe—and I'm getting—really scared," he said.

"Stay right where you are. I'm hanging up and calling 911. I'll be home just as soon as I can."

. . . .

DISPATCHER: "Request for first aid at 382 Bergen Street for a 15-year-old male with difficulty breathing."

"Yikes!" Archie said. "Hope the poor kid didn't run out of his medicine again."

When we arrived at the address, we discovered that Rod hadn't run out of medication after all. "The inhalers aren't helping," he said, obviously frightened as he struggled to get air into his lungs. "I called my mom. She called 911."

I noticed he was keeping his sentences very short, which is a telltale sign of true respiratory distress. "You did the right thing to call your mom," I said as I prepared the oxygen tank. "Try to take nice deep breaths in through your nose and out through your mouth so you get the oxygen." I adjusted the mask strap so it was a little tighter. I was concerned he hadn't improved after using his inhalers. Helen checked the expiration dates on them, but both were fine.

Similar to the last time we treated Rod, his pulse ox was low, and his heart rate was high. We moved him rapidly to our ambulance, where we met up with William and Rose. "We're going to give you a breathing treatment just like last time," Rose said as she efficiently administered the medication.

"I still can't breathe. Why can't I breathe?" Rod's hands were clenched tightly on the cot handrails, his knuckles turning white from squeezing so hard.

"Your lungs are sounding clearer already. Just give the medication a few minutes to work. Hang in there, buddy," William said.

"I just got word from dispatch that Rod's mom is going to meet us at the hospital. She'll probably beat us there," Archie called back to us from the driver's seat.

I could see that as Rod heard Archie's words, his grip on the handrails relaxed ever so slightly. By the time we arrived at the hospital, his breathing had noticeably improved. Although he seemed to be out of danger for the moment, he needed a thorough medical checkup with an allergist or pulmonologist to determine why his asthma appeared to be worsening.

· · · · · · · · · · · · · ·

One year later

> **DISPATCHER:** "Request for first aid at 382 Bergen Street for a 16-year-old male with an asthma attack."

Colleen climbed into the driver's seat. "We haven't had a call there in a long time. I was hoping he was doing better."

I jumped into the front passenger seat. "Me too. I figured no news is good news."

After Helen and Archie hopped in, we took off for Bergen Street.

> **DISPATCHER:** "Update for first aid call at 382 Bergen Street. Expedite. Patient with severe difficulty breathing."

Colleen took it up a notch, pushing down on the accelerator and turning on the ambulance's sirens. "Not good. He was pretty bad last time," she muttered.

"Yes, he really worried me last time. I remember it like it was yesterday," Helen said.

Archie nodded his head. "Frightening for both him and his mother."

> **DISPATCHER:** "Update for first aid call at 382 Bergen Street. As per patrols on scene, CPR is now in progress."

I felt the color drain from my face, and my heart started racing. I glanced at Colleen, who seemed like she wasn't faring much better.

I could hear screaming even before I got out of the ambulance, and I couldn't quite suppress a shiver. *Rod's mother. I can't even imagine what she's going through at this moment.*

We sprinted along the sidewalk with our equipment in hand. Helen threw open the front door, and we rushed inside. We followed the sound of Shirley's sobbing to Rod's bedroom on the second floor. The scene before us made my blood run cold, with the full horror of what I had feared in the ambulance now a harsh reality in front of me. As Officers McGovern and Endicott performed CPR, Shirley knelt by Rod's head, her hands stroking his hair. Colleen took her by the hand and led her toward the hallway.

"The difficulty breathing started out of the blue while he was in bed watching TV," Officer Endicott said. "He called his mom and used his inhaler, but it didn't help. He got progressively worse, and she called 911."

"He had agonal respirations when we got here," Officer McGovern added. "We started CPR right away. We put on the defibrillator, but so far, no shocks have been advised."

I knelt down and began performing chest compressions to give Officer McGovern a rest. Helen inserted an oral airway. Then she assisted Officer Endicott with providing respirations by tilting Rod's head back to maintain his airway in an open position.

Pretend it's just a drill. That this is not a real person. But it didn't work. I knew it was Rod. I knew it wasn't just a drill. I knew he was very much a real person.

We briefly paused with compressions and ventilations to let Archie slide a backboard under Rod. The defibrillator reanalyzed his heart rhythm. I cringed when the machine announced that no shock was advised. I tried not to look at Rod directly, but I couldn't seem to help it. He appeared so young, so helpless, so defenseless.

William and Rose arrived and did everything in their power to restore Rod's heartbeat. But it was not to be. Forty minutes later, his life on earth officially came to an end when the emergency room physician pronounced him deceased.

. . . .

The time came when the beggar died and the angels carried him to Abraham's side.

LUKE 16:22

In this verse from Luke, we learn that when the beggar named Lazarus died, the angels carried him away. I think in much the same way, angels guided Rod's spirit to heaven after his death.

I grieved for both Rod and his mother. A boy whose life was cut incredibly short by asthma. A mother, who would miss her son immeasurably. I've learned in my years as a volunteer emergency medical technician that sometimes there simply is no easy answer to the question, "Why, God?" This was one of those calls.

Dear Lord, please be with Shirley Blackwell as she struggles to accept her son's death. May she find peace on earth until the day when she is reunited with her son in heaven.

16

The Attack

Turn your ear to me,
come quickly to my rescue;
be my rock of refuge,
a strong fortress to save me.

PSALM 31:2

What should I do? Should I go back to Albert's house and check on him? Floyd Elliott paused indecisively in the middle of aisle 4 of the local hardware store. He needed to buy some fluorescent light bulbs as well as a few other small items, like superglue and nails. But now here he stood, consumed with the strangest feeling that he should go check on his friend Albert Baylor. The odd thing was he'd seen him not 30 minutes ago. The pair had gone out to lunch at a wharf-side restaurant, and then Floyd had dropped off Albert at his home. He'd waited until Albert had unlocked his front door and gone inside before he pulled away.

Floyd continued to ponder his dilemma while he stood in line to pay for his items. Once he settled into his car, he knew he wouldn't be able to have peace of mind until he saw that Albert was indeed okay.

Ten minutes later, Floyd parked under the shade of an elm tree in front of Albert's place, a small red ranch house on a quiet tree-lined street. Albert had lived there for at least 50 years—as long as Floyd had known him. Albert's wife had passed away about ten years before, so he lived alone now. *It's a good thing we've been friends for such a long time, because he's going to think I'm nuts for coming back so quickly.*

Floyd took off his sunglasses and tossed them onto the front passenger seat. He rang the doorbell, hearing the familiar sound of chimes through the heavy oak door. After a minute, when Albert didn't open the door, he rang the bell again.

Floyd's sense of unease grew as the seconds ticked by. Turning around, he glanced at the driveway and noted that Albert's small blue sedan was indeed still parked there. Floyd didn't own a cell phone. He briefly contemplated driving home and trying to call Albert but then decided against it.

He recalled that Albert kept a house key under his potted plant, so he slid his hand under the planter and pulled out a dirty key. Brushing it off, he inserted it into the keyhole. However, before he even turned the key, he realized the door was unlocked. His sense of disquiet increased even more. Albert was extremely cautious about safety. He *always* kept his door locked.

Floyd pushed the door open, his stomach now tied in knots. "Albert? Are you here? It's me." The house remained silent until a cuckoo clock robustly announced the hour.

Floyd jumped at the noise, his heart beginning to race. He hesitated briefly but then stepped further into the foyer. The shades were drawn, making the room rather dark. When he reached over and flipped the wall switch to turn on the lights, he almost keeled over at the sight that met him. There, on the foyer floor just outside the bathroom, lay a bloody knife!

Swallowing his panic, Floyd crept closer to the bathroom. Bracing himself, he peeked through the partially open door.

His dear friend lay crumpled in a pool of blood on the bathroom floor. He knelt next to Albert and shook his shoulder. "Can you hear me?" When Albert failed to respond, Floyd raced over to the phone in the kitchen and dialed the police department.

"Pine Cove Police Department. This is Dispatcher Franklin. How can I help you?"

"My friend. He's been attacked. There's blood everywhere. He's not moving at all. I'm afraid he might be—" Floyd couldn't finish his sentence.

"Sir, where are you right now?" Dispatcher Franklin asked.

"I'm on Chambers Street. Number 461."

"You said that someone attacked your friend. Do you think that the attacker might still be in the house?"

"I'm not sure. I suppose he could be." Floyd's eyes grew large with fear as he looked down the hallways and into the living room. "I didn't think of that. I was so worried about Albert."

"I know you want to help your friend, but I need to keep you safe. I want you to leave the home until the patrolmen arrive, okay? Meet them out front. I'm sending the police and an ambulance right now."

. . . .

DISPATCHER: "Request for first aid at 461 Chambers Street. Remain outside in your ambulance until the scene is declared safe. The call is for an assault victim."

Greg Turner arrived at the first aid building first and started up the ambulance. Greg, an electrical engineer, began volunteering with our department several years earlier. Both intelligent and compassionate, I thought he made an excellent addition to our squad. "This doesn't sound good," he remarked as I climbed in next to him.

"Yes, it sounds serious. I guess the police are securing the scene right now." I was grateful that we had an exemplary police department to make sure we stayed safe.

Ted O'Malley parked his car across the street from the first aid building and hurried over to the ambulance. He slid onto the bench in the rear of the ambulance. "I heard on my scanner that they may have a possible suspect in the home."

DISPATCHER: "Update for 461 Chambers Street. The scene is now safe. Expedite. Patient is an unconscious elderly male with profuse bleeding."

"I'll get the trauma kit," Ted said as we arrived on location. "Andrea, can you grab the first aid bag?"

After reaching into the side compartment to pull out our first aid kit, I noticed an older man in a red plaid shirt nervously wringing his hands in front of the house. He rushed over to us and grabbed my arm, pulling me toward the home. "Please, do something quick. My friend's in terrible shape. I've never seen so much blood."

When I stepped into the foyer, I smelled the blood before I saw it. It was a strong metallic smell, like a cup of change that has been sitting in a hot car all day. I stopped breathing through my nose and switched to my mouth.

"Our patient is Albert Baylor, approximate age 75," Sergeant Flint said. "His friend Floyd reports he dropped him off after lunch about forty minutes ago. He came back to check on him and found him like this. There was a bloody knife found in the foyer, not far from where the patient is lying."

Officer Sims strung yellow crime scene tape across the front door. "Until we know exactly what we're dealing with, we need to treat this as a crime scene. I need to keep curious neighbors out."

Ted, Greg, and I nodded and headed toward the bathroom. I was shocked by the sight of so much blood. It covered the patient, the walls, the floor, the sink, and even the counter. Greg and I squeezed into the small room while Ted hovered close to the doorway. There was so much blood that initially it was hard to pinpoint where it was all coming from.

Sergeant Flint and Officer Sims had already placed Mr. Baylor on high-flow oxygen. I squatted down near him and tried to feel his radial pulse. His entire wrist was covered in thick, sticky blood, and I was grateful for my vinyl gloves. *No radial pulse. That means his systolic blood pressure must be less than 80 mm Hg.* I rolled up his sleeve and applied a blood pressure cuff. I figured I wouldn't be able to hear the blood pressure because it would be too low, but I tried anyway. I couldn't hear it, so I repumped the cuff and felt for his pulse.

"BP is 76 by palpation," I said to Ted, who was standing in the doorway with the clipboard. When we take a blood pressure by palpation (releasing pressure from the cuff and determining when we first feel the pulse) instead of by auscultation (listening with a stethoscope), there is only a systolic number (which is the top number in blood pressure readings). "His pulse is very weak. He's probably in hemorrhagic shock." I listened to his lungs and was relieved to note that they were equal and bilateral, indicating he didn't have a sucking chest wound.

Greg pulled some thick dressings, roller gauze, and tape out of our trauma kit. "I've rinsed the wounds with sterile water, and it looks like they are mainly on his wrists and abdomen."

"Let's focus on those, and then we can roll him over and check his back." I held down the dressings while Greg applied roller gauze and tape to hold them in place.

When Sergeant Flint poked his head in to check on Albert, we explained the location of the wounds.

"It sounds like they could be self-inflicted," Sergeant Flint said.

Ted jotted down some more notes on the patient report. "That's what I was thinking."

Floyd, who was standing in the foyer close to the bathroom, overheard our conversation. "Self-inflicted? That's impossible."

"Think back to your lunch together today. Did Albert act unusual at all?" Sergeant Flint asked.

Floyd pondered the question, and his face clouded over. "Well, now that I think of it, something about him did seem off."

"Did he mention feeling depressed?" I asked.

"Not outright, no. I can't put a finger on it exactly, but he did seem a little bit down in the dumps."

We rolled Albert onto a collapsible stretcher to maneuver him out of the tiny bathroom and onto our stretcher in the foyer. I was relieved to note that there were no knife wounds on his back. Albert let out a soft moan, but his eyes remained closed.

"I'm not going to let him come home to the house looking like this. Are there professional cleaning services that specialize in cases like this?" Floyd asked.

"Yes. But first we need to finish investigating the scene. I can get you information on cleaning companies later," Sergeant Flint replied.

Paramedics Ty Fleming and Paula Pritchard arrived as we loaded Albert into our ambulance. They quickly established an IV line to address his dangerously low blood pressure. Fortunately, the bleeding from his knife wounds dramatically decreased after we bandaged him.

As we traveled to the hospital, I reflected on how it was truly a blessing that Floyd Elliott went back to Albert Baylor's home to check on him. If he hadn't, Albert could very likely have died that day. We later learned that Albert made a full recovery from his injuries. I prayed that with proper counseling and support from family and friends, he would heal emotionally as well.

. . . .

While I was speaking and praying, confessing my sin and the sin of my people Israel and making my request to the LORD my God for his holy hill—while I was still in prayer, Gabriel, the man I had seen in the earlier vision, came to me in swift flight about the time of the evening sacrifice. He instructed me and said to me, "Daniel, I have now come to give you insight and understanding. As soon as you began to pray, a word went out, which I have come to tell you, for you are highly esteemed. Therefore, consider the word and understand the vision:

"Seventy 'sevens' are decreed for your people and your holy city to finish transgression, to put an end to sin, to atone for wickedness, to bring in everlasting righteousness, to seal up vision and prophecy and to anoint the Most Holy Place."

DANIEL 9:20-24

Have you ever had an episode like Floyd Elliott in which you felt compelled to check on someone? An experience you couldn't explain? A dream that seemed so vivid it felt real? Sometimes, things happen to us that don't have an easy explanation. That's where faith comes in.

As a physical therapist, I work closely with my patients and grow to care about them. One morning at about 4:30 a.m., I awoke from a bad dream I was having about one of my outpatients. (I'll call her "Jess.") In my dream, Jess was lying on one of our treatment tables. She became very pale, and her skin turned cool and clammy. I noticed something was wrong with her eyes; she appeared to be staring sightlessly. I immediately ran across the gym to a telephone and called 911. When I returned, she began to come around. After a few minutes, she was okay.

The dream left me very unsettled, and I was anxious to see Jess later that morning at her physical therapy appointment to make sure she was all right. The time for her therapy session came and went, and my sense of disquiet grew. The front office staff told me she had called and canceled therapy for the day, but they weren't sure why.

Early the next week, Jess arrived for her next scheduled physical therapy appointment. I joked that she was invading my dreams and confided I'd had a bad dream about her.

Jess looked startled. "What was the dream?"

I explained about the medical episode, including her pale, cool, clammy skin and her blank stare.

"What time was your dream?" she asked.

"About 4:30. It woke me up, and I didn't go back to sleep." I normally wake up for work at five.

Jess went on to explain that at 4:30 on the morning she canceled therapy, she had experienced a low blood sugar emergency. She awoke not feeling well and had cool, clammy skin. She walked into the bathroom, and when she looked into the mirror, she realized she was having trouble seeing. She immediately ate some food and candy, and she felt better. Jess isn't a diabetic, but she explained that her doctor said one of her medications was interfering with her blood sugar levels.

I'm not sure how to explain what happened that morning. One of my friends suggested that our guardian angels must have connected. I told my patient we must be soul sisters.

17

The Hero

*As for me, I call to God,
and the LORD saves me.
Evening, morning and noon
I cry out in distress,
and he hears my voice.*

PSALM 55:16-17

While waiting for the train, Rita Robertson pulled her novel out of her purse and quickly buried her nose in it. A compulsive reader, she'd just begun the last chapter and was desperate to discover how it ended. Completely engrossed in her book and unaware of the crowd around her, she didn't notice when she stepped across the yellow warning line on the platform and moved dangerously close to the six-foot drop to the subway tracks. Lost in the action of her novel, she took one step backward, but then two frontward. The second step sent her pitching headfirst to the tracks below.

. . . .

"What a fun day," my friend Hope said as we made our way onto the subway platform. My sister Marie and I were visiting her for a week, and the three of us had just spent a fun day shopping and going to a ball game. The platform began filling with people, so we meandered closer to the front of the crowd. Suddenly, I heard an odd thudding noise, and the people around us surged forward. A woman close by began screaming, her shrieks sending goose bumps down my spine.

"I wonder what's going on?" Marie asked.

No sooner had she uttered the words than a man yelled out, "Help! There's a woman on the tracks."

The three of us pushed our way forward, closer to the train tracks. My jaw dropped open in shock when I noticed a young woman lying face down, unconscious on the tracks below.

"The train's due any minute," someone nearby shouted.

I knew I wasn't strong enough to jump down onto the tracks, pick up a woman the same size as me, and lift her up over my head to the platform. Even if I jumped down, I wouldn't be able to pull myself back up again.

A hushed silence fell over the anxious crowd. Precious seconds ticked by as the woman continued to lie motionless on the tracks. If she didn't move very, very soon, she would most certainly die.

In moments such as this, heroes are born. They are the ones who selflessly put their lives on the line for another. They risk everything to save someone else.

That day a hero *was* born. A tall, muscular man burst to the front of the crowd and leapt onto the tracks. He raced over to the woman and shook her shoulders. "Wake up!" he shouted urgently. She moaned in response but didn't awaken. With herculean strength, the man hoisted her onto his shoulder and carried her across the tracks to the platform's edge.

"Hurry!" several people yelled. In the distance, the wailing train whistle warned of impending doom.

"I'm going to faint," I heard a woman somewhere behind me declare, but I didn't turn to look. My eyes were focused on the man and woman before us. At that precise moment, an amazing thing happened. As a group, we and all the people around us surged toward the woman and her rescuer. Dozens of hands grabbed their arms, hands, legs, and even the clothing on their backs…virtually anything they could grip.

The whistle grew louder as the train drew closer. In what seemed like an eternity, but was probably only a few seconds, our hodgepodge team of rescuers pulled the two up to safety. The crowd let out a collective sigh of relief.

As heroes often do, the man simply smiled and melted away into the crowd. The train pulled into the station, and the people around us poured into it. Hope, Marie, and I stayed behind to help the woman, who was now conscious and lying on the ground about eight feet from the platform.

"Hi, I'm Andrea, and I'm an emergency medical technician. Someone called the police, and they're on the way. What's your name?" I asked, trying to get a feel for her mental condition.

"My name is Rita. What just happened?" she whispered.

"You fell onto the tracks. A man jumped down and lifted you up," I replied.

"I don't remember. It's all a blur. I just know I was reading my book."

"Does anything hurt?" I asked. "You were knocked unconscious when you fell."

Rita rubbed her forehead. "Yes, my head hurts. Where's my purse? And my book?"

Marie peered over the edge of the platform. "I'm afraid they may still be on the tracks."

Just then, the transit police arrived along with an EMS team, and they took over the care of Rita. Hope, Marie, and I said our goodbyes and wished her a speedy recovery. Rita probably wouldn't find out the ending to her book right away, but now she had a chance to create new chapters in her own life story.

· · · · · · · · · · · · · ·

Do you think I cannot call on my Father, and he will at once put at my disposal more than twelve legions of angels?

MATTHEW 26:53

This verse from Matthew underscores the fact that there are not a mere one or two angels in heaven, but legions of angels. A legion is generally considered to be at least several thousand—possibly 6,000. So, if we do the math, God could send out more than 72,000 angels!

Angels are strong, as evidenced in Scripture (for example, see Psalm 103:20; Matthew 28:2-7; Acts 5:19; 12:7,23; 2 Thessalonians 1:7; 2 Peter 2:11; and Revelation 5:2). On the day that Rita fell onto the tracks, I have no doubt that many people in the crowd were earnestly praying for her rescue.

Although angels are spirits (Hebrews 1:14), they can appear as men (Genesis 19:1-3; Daniel 8:15; 10:16,18; and Hebrews 13:2). Could the man who rescued Rita have been a guardian angel?

18

The Stroke

Those who look to him are radiant;
their faces are never covered with shame.
This poor man called, and the LORD heard him;
he saved him out of all his troubles.

PSALM 34:5-6

Clara West stared at herself in the bathroom mirror. *The left side of my face looks droopy.* She touched her left cheek, wrinkled by years of too much sun and smoking when she was young. Next, she touched her right cheek. It seemed to her as though she could feel her touch better on the right side than on the left.

When her husband, Clarence, was still alive, she had taken him to a neurologist after he'd had a stroke. Now, she tried to recall some of the tests the doctor had performed. *Smile and stick out your tongue.* She tried to smile, but the left side of her face wouldn't cooperate. Then she tried to stick out her tongue, but her tongue wouldn't do what she wanted it to either. Clara tried to smile again, and this time, she had no problem whatsoever. Puzzled, she tried to stick out her tongue and was able to do that too. *What in the world is going on?*

Shrugging her shoulders, she flipped off the bathroom light and wandered back into the family room. Curling up on the sofa, she reached over and picked up one of her magazines. She thumbed through the pages but couldn't fully concentrate. Her mind kept wandering back to the episode in the bathroom.

Putting down her magazine, she reached for a glass of water. As Clara took a sip, she suddenly felt an odd buzzing sensation on the left side of her face. Frowning, she returned to the bathroom and stared for a second time at her reflection in the mirror. *The left side of my face is drooping again.* Once more, she tried to see if she could smile normally, but only the right side of her face curved into a smile. The left side remained stubbornly droopy.

I suppose I should go to the hospital and get checked out. It will have to be Montgomery Hospital, since Clarence used to be on the board of trustees there.

. . . .

DISPATCHER: "Request for first aid at 871 Crestview Drive for a woman having a possible stroke."

Magnificent weeping willows lined the driveway of a breathtaking white Colonial with slate-blue shutters. As Jose Sanchez efficiently backed our ambulance down the long cobblestone drive, I couldn't help but notice how the gracious branches of the willows gently stroked the roof and sides of our ambulance, as if welcoming us. After Jose finished parking, he, Ted O'Malley, and I made our way up a steep flight of porch steps to a large wraparound veranda. The front door was wide open, so we stepped inside.

"Hello, first aid squad," Ted called out.

"Up the stairs and to the right," Officer Endicott responded.

We hurried up a large, sweeping staircase to a second-floor sitting room. An older woman with an elegantly coiffed updo sat on the edge of a burgundy wing chair, close to an ornate brick fireplace.

Officer Endicott introduced us to our patient. "This is Clara West, age 80. In the past thirty minutes, she's had two episodes of left facial drooping, each of which lasted about two minutes or so. Her past medical history is significant for high blood pressure and a heart attack two years ago. I put her on oxygen at 15 liters per minute."

Clara smoothed a few loose strands of hair. "I really just need a ride to Montgomery Hospital. I feel perfectly fine right now."

"Bakersville Hospital is much closer. That's where we usually take people," I pointed out.

"My husband, when he was alive, was on the board of trustees at Montgomery Hospital. I know I'll get the best possible care there."

"It sounds as though you may be having TIAs," I said, referring to transient ischemic attacks. A TIA can be a warning sign that a larger stroke is imminent. "Bakersville Hospital has a top-notch stroke team."

"Thank you, but no. I'm going to Montgomery, and it's not open for discussion," Clara said firmly.

"You may want to reconsider," Jose said. "We rarely go to Montgomery because it's so far away. If you're having a stroke, Bakersville is truly the way to go."

"I appreciate your opinion. Now, if you don't mind, let's stop talking about it. I've already made my decision." Just as Clara finished speaking, she began to noticeably slur her words. At the same time, the left side of her face began drooping.

After checking the gauge on the portable oxygen tank, Ted knelt next to Clara and took her pulse and blood pressure. "Her blood pressure is 164 over 100, and her pulse is 104, strong and regular. Respirations are 16. Her lungs sound clear."

I jotted down the vital signs on our call sheet. Ted ran through a neurological assessment with Clara, including a "FAST" test, noting that her right grasp was a bit weak. A FAST test is a quick screening for a stroke. *F* stands for facial drooping, *A* for arm weakness, *S* for speech difficulty, and *T* means time to call 911.

By the time Ted was done assessing Clara, her facial droop had resolved again. "Let's get moving. We can meet the medics in the ambulance," he said.

Rose Anderson and William Moore arrived from the hospital just as Officer Endicott and Jose were maneuvering the stair chair down the front porch steps, so they set up their equipment in the ambulance.

I followed behind them and gave them our patient report. I explained Clara's determination to go to Montgomery Hospital, even though Bakersville was much closer.

"Not to worry. We'll change her mind," William said. "If she's had three TIAs in a half hour, she belongs in the closest hospital."

I swung open the rear doors to the ambulance. "Well, I hope you have better luck convincing her than we did, because here she comes."

"Good afternoon," William said, hooking Clara up to a heart monitor. "Before we get moving, I just wanted to say that I strongly advise you to go to the nearest hospital." He and Rose took turns explaining why Bakersville was the better choice in this case, but Clara turned a deaf ear to them.

"Please listen closely," she said. "I apologize if I seem rude, but I don't wish to say this again. I absolutely refuse to go anywhere except Montgomery. So, let's stop wasting time and get going or find me an ambulance that can take me where I want to go." Clara spoke like a person who was used to getting her own way, and her tone brooked no room for argument.

We gave up trying to change her mind and began the trip to Montgomery. About halfway there, Clara began slurring her words again, and the facial droop reappeared. She looked frightened. Frankly, I was frightened for her. *Four transient ischemic attacks in less than one hour. A very serious situation.*

The remainder of the trip passed uneventfully. When we arrived at Montgomery Hospital, the medics gave their report to the triage nurse, and we transferred care of Clara over to her.

· · · · · · · · · · · · ·

Several weeks later

"Is your headache any better?" Eddie McCourt asked his friend Mack Conley. He and Mack had been friends since grammar school. Today they had gone out for a late lunch at Webster's Bar and Grille, followed by a movie.

Mack adjusted his baseball cap so it shielded his eyes from the late afternoon sun. "No, it's still pretty bad. I'm going to take some ibuprofen as soon as I get home. I've been under the weather for a couple days now."

"It's more than a headache, you mean?" Eddie asked.

"Well, I've been a little queasy. I feel a bit unsteady on my feet. Let's just say I'm glad you're driving right now, not me. I think that chicken club sandwich may have made it worse."

"You shouldn't mess around with that kind of stuff. You said you were feeling bad before lunch, so I really don't think the chicken sandwich has anything to do with it. You should see your doctor if you don't feel well. Do you want me to take you to the emergency room?" Eddie knew Mack was the kind of person who delayed going to a physician until the last possible second. He once waited an entire month before caving in and seeking help for a terrible sinus infection.

Mack fumbled to release his seat belt. "Good grief, no. It's really not that bad. I'll be fine in the morning. But thank you. We're nearly at my house now. I plan on going to bed early."

Eddie capitulated. "Okay, but I'll see you in and make sure you get settled. Please call me right away if something changes."

"It won't, but I promise if it does, I will. I really do appreciate your concern."

Eddie pulled onto Mack's red brick driveway in front of a small one-car garage. As Eddie walked along the winding path to Mack's front door, he noticed that his friend staggered several times, though he was able to regain his balance.

"Here, let me get the door for you," Eddie said. Mack muttered something in reply, but it sounded garbled and unclear. Now thoroughly alarmed, Eddie put his arm around Mack and led him through the foyer. He wanted to get him sitting safely on the sofa so he could take a better look at him.

Mack veered toward the staircase that led to the second floor so quickly that Eddie could barely hold on to him.

"I think you should stay down here," Eddie said, concerned his friend wouldn't be able to safely climb the stairs. Mack shook him off, grabbed hold of the oak railing, and lunged up the stairs. When he reached the landing, his legs suddenly gave out, and he collapsed onto his left side.

Eddie knelt next to him. "What's wrong?"

Mack didn't answer.

"I'm going to get help right away." Jumping to his feet, Eddie rushed to the nearest phone and dialed 911.

. . . .

DISPATCHER: "Request for first aid at 202 Jefferson Avenue for a man who collapsed on the staircase."

"I'll drive," Darren Williams said, sliding behind the wheel.

Ted sat down next to him, and I climbed into the back of the ambulance and buckled up for the ride. A few minutes later, we pulled up in front of a small white clapboard house with a cozy front portico. A large Boston fern hung to the left of the entrance, its long fronds waving gently in the breeze.

When I stepped inside, I was surprised to see my friend Eddie McCourt rushing toward us. I had just run into him earlier that afternoon when we had responded to a first aid call at Webster's Bar and Grille. A lady had choked on a piece of steak, and a waiter gave her the Heimlich maneuver. She ended up signing a refusal form and stayed to finish her meal. On our way out, I had run into Eddie, and he had introduced me to his friend Mack Conley. I knew Eddie lived on the other side of town, so I wasn't sure why he was here on Jefferson Avenue.

"It's my friend Mack, the man I introduced you to today at lunch," Eddie began. "He said he hasn't felt good for the past few days and has had a headache. I brought him inside, and suddenly his voice started to sound funny, like he was slurring his words. Then he collapsed on the stairs. Now it seems like he can't move the right side of his body." Eddie motioned us to follow him and led us down a short hallway to a flight of stairs.

My mind flashed to Clara West, the woman who had suffered

multiple transient ischemic attacks several weeks earlier. As dire as her situation had seemed at the time, Mack's seemed much worse. As I passed through the foyer and faced the stairs, I saw Officer Sims kneeling next to an older gentleman with a full head of silver-white hair.

Officer Sims unfolded his long legs. "It's tight quarters here. I'll get out of the way so you can do your assessment. I put him on high-flow oxygen."

I sat down on the step next to Mr. Conley. "I'm Andrea from the Pine Cove First Aid Squad. I'm a friend of Eddie McCourt. I met you earlier today when you were having lunch at Webster's. Can you tell me how you feel right now?"

Mack tried to turn toward me, his eyes wide with fear. "I have a really bad headache, and I can't move this side." He tried to move his right arm and leg but failed to do so. His words were slurred together and spoken so softly that it was difficult to understand him.

I quickly performed an assessment as best as I could within the cramped confines of the staircase. "Blood pressure is 204 over 108, heart rate is 110, and respiratory rate is 20," I said to Darren, who was preparing the call sheet. "His lungs sound clear. He has facial asymmetry with decreased strength and sensation on the right side."

As we worked as a team to get a collapsible stretcher under Mack, he grabbed my forearm with his left hand. "Please, help me."

"We're taking you to Bakersville Hospital right now. They'll take excellent care of you," I promised. It was good that Mack's friend had witnessed his collapse. If Mack was having an embolic stroke (an ischemic stroke caused by a clot in which blood flow becomes restricted to the involved area of the brain), it was imperative to get him to the hospital as soon as possible for life-saving medications such as tPA (tissue plasminogen activator).

The window for administering tPA is quite small. To benefit from it, a patient must receive it within three hours from the onset of the stroke (or, in certain special situations, within four and a half hours). It works by dissolving the clot and increasing blood flow to the ischemic area. However, hospital staff can't just give it to anyone who presents stroke-like symptoms. First, the patient must undergo testing to determine what kind of stroke they are having. For example, if the patient is having a hemorrhagic stroke (a brain bleed), then the use of tPA is contraindicated because it could worsen his or her condition.

"I'm going to leave now and drive straight to the hospital," Eddie said. "I'll meet you in the emergency room."

I briefly nodded before turning my attention back to Mack.

Medics William and Rose met us in the foyer. "We'll do our assessment in the ambulance," Rose said.

As Darren and Ted strapped Mack onto our stretcher, I picked up our first aid bag and followed the paramedics out to our rig.

"Do you remember the woman we took up a few weeks ago who had the ministrokes?" I asked.

"Sure do. She had a massive stroke about two hours after we dropped her off at the hospital," Rose replied.

"Did she make it?" I asked, even though I could already tell the answer from Rose's face.

"No, she died instantly," William said. "I mean, they worked on her for a while, but they were never able to bring her back."

In light of this news, my concern for Mack grew. I sat down next to him on the bench in the back of the ambulance and held his hand the entire trip to the hospital. I hoped the gesture would bring him at least a small measure of comfort as he faced the uncertainty ahead.

The stroke team met us in the emergency department, and within mere minutes, Mack was being rushed off for a CT scan of his brain. I knew the next hours would prove crucial for a possible recovery.

. . . .

My phone rang early the next morning. I recognized Eddie McCourt's voice right away, and I found myself hoping that he was calling with good news about his friend Mack.

"He made it through the night, and he's doing a little better," Eddie said.

I was thankful Mack had survived the stroke. Once again, I found myself thinking of Clara West. *We never truly know when the Lord will call us home.*

. . . .

Peter followed him out of the prison, but he had no idea that what the angel was doing was really happening; he thought he was seeing a vision. They passed the first and second guards and came to the iron gate leading to the city. It opened for them by itself, and they went through it. When they had walked the length of one street, suddenly the angel left him.

Then Peter came to himself and said, "Now I know without a doubt that the Lord has sent his angel and rescued me from Herod's clutches and from everything the Jewish people were hoping would happen."

ACTS 12:9-11

Years ago, one of my dear friends passed away. (I'll call him "Roger.") That night, I sat on the edge of my bed crying and said aloud, "Roger, I love you and miss you."

The doorbell rang. My husband, Rick, and I exchanged surprised looks. Who would be ringing our doorbell at 11 o'clock on a weeknight? We decided to go downstairs and look together. When my husband opened our front door, no one was there. At the time, we lived in a house with a long driveway. There was no way someone could ring the bell and walk away without being seen.

"Wait a second," Rick said. "That was the old doorbell that rang." He had installed a new doorbell system earlier that week. The new doorbell was wired to ring our house telephone. But it had most definitely been the old doorbell chime we both had heard.

"That's odd. Where's our old doorbell?"

Rick pulled the old doorbell out of an end table drawer in our family room. *It had no batteries in it!*

"Wait a second. Let me get this straight. I said, 'Roger, I love you and miss you.' Then we both heard our old doorbell ring. We came downstairs, looked outside, and no one was there.

Now we check our old doorbell, and it's a piece of plastic with no batteries inside. How is that possible?"

But even as I asked the question, I think I knew the answer. Roger had witnessed my heartfelt tears and given me a small sign to show he was okay. It was just the kind of caring thing he would do. Could an angel have somehow helped him? The ringing of the doorbell brought me immeasurable comfort and affirmed my belief in the afterlife.

19

Heroin or Heroine

*The salvation of the righteous comes from the L*ORD*;*
he is their stronghold in time of trouble.
*The L*ORD *helps them and delivers them;*
he delivers them from the wicked and saves them,
because they take refuge in him.

PSALM 37:39-40

D ispatcher Jerome Franklin answered the phone. "Pine Cove Police. Do you have an emergency?"

"Hi, this is Eleanor Whitley, Sasha Whitley's mother. She lives in Pine Cove Apartments, and she's not answering her phone. I'm worried because I can't drive at night, so I can't go over to check on her."

"Do you have a reason to think she may be in danger?" Dispatcher Franklin asked.

"Well, yes. She's a recovering heroin addict. She just got out of rehab a few days ago. I was hoping that perhaps one of your officers could go to her apartment and check on her."

"Of course. What's her apartment number?"

"Building 4, apartment A. Thank you so much," Eleanor replied.

"I'll be in touch. Can I reach you at this number?"

"Yes. I hope she's okay."

. . . .

"We've been to this apartment before. If it's the same girl, she's only 26 or 27. I think her name is Sasha," Colleen Harper noted.

"What a shame. People dig themselves into such a deep hole, and I guess it's awfully hard for them to find their way back out," Alec Waters mused.

"Hopefully she'll kick the habit sooner rather than later. Heroin really messes with a person," Archie Harris chimed in.

When we arrived at the apartment complex and hustled toward building 4, I noticed the late autumn sun did little to take the chill out of the air. Shivering, I zipped up my jacket a little higher. However, as I stepped across the threshold into apartment A, a warm blast of stale air assaulted me. I quickly unzipped my coat again.

Sergeant Flint was kneeling next to a young woman with long dark hair. He supported her at the shoulders so she would stay on her left side. "I'm going to need an emesis basin right away." He brushed some of the girl's hair away from her cheek. "I'm pretty sure she's about to vomit."

"Is that Sasha under all that hair?" Colleen asked.

"Yes. Her mother called us to do a welfare check. She just got out of drug rehab a few days ago." Sergeant Flint pointed to a small pine table next to a sleeper sofa. "I found drug paraphernalia on the end table."

It looked as though Sasha had been lying on the sofa and, at some point, inadvertently rolled onto the floor. Gaunt cheeks and dark black circles under her eyes contributed to an overall poor appearance.

"The medics are three minutes out," Archie said.

At the time, police and EMS units didn't carry naloxone (also known by the brand name Narcan) to reverse the effects of narcotic drug overdoses; we had to wait for the paramedics. Nowadays, trained police and EMS can administer nasal naloxone if a patient meets certain criteria, such as exhibiting a poor respiratory rate (less than ten breaths per minute) with pinpoint pupils, a witnessed overdose by bystanders, past medical history of narcotic/opioid drug use, or narcotic/opioid drug paraphernalia at the scene. Sasha already met two of these criteria (history of abuse and drug paraphernalia present), so I knew she would be a candidate for naloxone.

Although Sasha moaned as she emptied the contents of her stomach into a basin, she remained largely unresponsive.

"Blood pressure 106 over 78. Heart rate 106 and regular. Respirations 12." Colleen shined a penlight into Sasha's eyes. "She has pinpoint pupils, which are nonreactive to light. Her skin is cool and clammy." Since Sasha appeared to be done vomiting, at least for the moment, Colleen put the oxygen mask back on her face.

There was a brief knock on the apartment door, and paramedics Ty Fleming and Paula Pritchard stepped inside. "Oh, I recognize her," Paula said right away. "I think I was here a few months ago. Heroin, right?"

I nodded. "She just got out of rehab a few days ago." I gave the patient report to Ty as Paula started an IV line.

Paula injected the naloxone intravenously. "This shouldn't take long."

I watched in amazement as Sasha "woke up." She pushed herself up with her arms and sat up straight, then rested her back against the sofa. She scowled fiercely at the sight of our faces. "What are you doing here? I'm perfectly fine. Everything's under control."

"Your mother called us and asked us to check on you," Sergeant Flint replied. "She couldn't reach you by phone and was really worried about you."

Although Sasha tried to hide it, a guilty look flashed briefly across her face, and her shoulders hunched forward a bit. "Oh," she said, suddenly at a loss for words.

It seemed to me as though Sasha should go straight back to rehab after a trip to the emergency room. I was glad she had a supportive mother. I prayed that one day she would be able to pull herself together. She was much too young to waste her life on drugs.

• • • • • • • • • • • • •

Several months later

The demons were chasing her again. They were relentless, terrorizing her days and haunting her dreams at night. She simply had to get away from them. But how? *Run. Run as fast as you can.* Not bothering to even put on a pair of shoes, she threw open the apartment door and rushed out into the parking lot. She hesitated only once to glance behind her. *They're chasing me. Why won't they leave me alone?* Panting now, she ran as hard as she could.

Focused on her flight, she didn't stop to look for traffic on the road in front of her apartment complex. Instead, she darted straight through the tall evergreen hedge that surrounded the complex and hurled herself onto the roadway.

• • • • • • • • • • • • •

At the tender age of 17, Timmy Johnson was a brand-new driver. His mother had just started letting him take her car out for brief trips after dark. He glanced at the dashboard clock. Timmy was a good kid, a straight-A student, and very conscientious. Careful to maintain the speed limit, he hummed to himself as he headed toward home.

Something in his peripheral vision suddenly caught his attention. Startled, he slammed violently on his brakes, hoping that whatever it was wouldn't dash out into the road. He continued pressing as hard as he could on the brake pedal, but it was no use. Timmy smashed hard into the person, the sheer force throwing him backward in his seat. Almost like a scene out of a horror movie, the body was flung up onto his hood, across his windshield, and then into the middle of the road. Quickly turning off the car, Timmy raced toward the victim, who now lay face down on the asphalt. Hands shaking violently, he pulled his cell phone out of his jacket pocket and dialed 911.

• • • • • • • • • • • • •

DISPATCHER: "Request for first aid in front of Pine Cove Apartments for a struck female pedestrian. Patient is unconscious with a severe head injury. Expedite."

Our ambulance whizzed toward the accident scene. "I hope it's not Sasha," I said.

"We haven't had a call for her for several months. I was hoping she went back to rehab and is doing better," Colleen said.

My heart sank as we pulled up in front of Pine Cove Apartments. From a distance, I saw a whole bunch of long, dark hair.

Colleen saw the hair right away too. "It sure looks like it might be her."

I passed by a young man with an ashen-white face who stood near a small sport utility vehicle. The police had already closed the road to traffic, and his was the only car parked close by. It wasn't too hard to put two and two together. I figured he must be the one who hit her. I wished I could stop to see if he was okay, but I knew that would have to wait.

Alec had gone directly to the accident scene. He was kneeling at the young woman's head, keeping her airway open with a modified jaw thrust technique to protect her cervical spine. "I need trauma dressings right away. There's a lot of blood coming from the back of her head."

I noticed that fluid was leaking from the woman's ears and realized she might have a skull fracture. Although the darkness and blood made it challenging to see, I had a sinking feeling that the young woman who lay unconscious on the ground was indeed Sasha.

"Let me give you some light," Helen McGuire said, directing a large flashlight onto the victim's face. I realized with relief that it wasn't Sasha after all, though she certainly could have passed for a relative.

"Her Glasgow score is only a 3," Alec said. Since she had the lowest possible score on the trauma assessment scale for acute brain injuries, we knew her situation was very critical.

The next few minutes passed in a blur of activity as Alec, Colleen, Archie, and a host of other squad members worked together to control the woman's bleeding, assist her breathing with a bag valve mask, and stabilize her spine with a collar and backboard. Alec and Archie lifted the backboard up onto our stretcher and began quickly rolling it toward our ambulance. I stooped to pick up some bloody dressings and other first aid related garbage from the road.

As I stood up, Sergeant Flint approached and said, "We've got a possible first name for the woman—Kayla—though we're working on confirming it. If it's her, she has a history of heroin abuse. Did she regain consciousness?" He'd been busy working on the accident investigation and hadn't been involved with patient care.

"No. It looks pretty grim. I think she may have a very severe head injury," I replied.

"Let them know at the hospital that I'll be up shortly, okay?"

I nodded and headed over to our ambulance. On the way there, I passed the young man who had accidentally struck Kayla. I was glad to see a middle-aged woman had her arm around his shoulder, comforting him. I figured it was probably his mother. I hoped she would help him recover emotionally from the tragic experience.

Glancing through the rear window of the ambulance, I could see that Ty and Paula were already inside, intubating Kayla and starting an IV line. Opening the door a crack, I stuck my head inside and relayed the information from Sergeant Flint that the victim may be a heroin user. But in my heart, I didn't think all the naloxone in the world was going to help her. Her problem was much bigger: one of the worst traumatic brain injuries I've ever seen.

. . . .

"I heard that she's not expected to make it through the night," Helen said after we'd finished the call.

"That's such a shame," Colleen said. "They think she was high on something. A witness said he saw her running across the parking lot and out into the road like she was being chased by the devil."

As it turned out, Kayla did live through the night. After several weeks in an induced coma, she was eventually transferred to a traumatic brain injury rehabilitation hospital. I prayed that with intensive rehab, she would one day be able to function independently again. And if she did, I hoped she would kick her drug problem once and for all.

My mind flashed to Sasha Whitley. I wished she'd also be able to defeat the demons that tortured her. I reflected on how the difference between heroin and heroine is only the letter *e*. If Sasha was able to kick her heroin habit, then she most certainly would be a heroine in my book.

. . . .

The devil left him, and angels came and attended him.

MATTHEW 4:11

Sasha Whitley, like so many people, struggled with her addiction to heroin. Every day, people struggle to turn away from temptation—whether it be food, alcohol, gambling, money, or even cheating on a significant other. Sometimes, we may need encouragement when we inadvertently enclose ourselves in a prison of our own making.

When Jesus was tempted by the devil, He turned away from Satan. Matthew 4:11 demonstrates that when we turn away from temptation and give ourselves to God, He may send angels to assist us.

20

No Medics!

The LORD sustains them on their sickbed
and restores them from their bed of illness.

PSALM 41:3

The shortness of breath came on so suddenly that it caught Red
Wakefield completely by surprise. He was no stranger to difficult
breathing; he'd already gone to the hospital three times due to congestive heart failure. The cardiologist said his heart valves didn't work well
anymore, but unfortunately, he wasn't a candidate for surgery. She
said that they'd have to treat his heart failure with medications instead.

Today started off like a typical day. A breakfast of oatmeal and a
banana. Reading the newspaper. Taking a walk around the block to get
a little exercise. Doing a crossword puzzle. Nothing too exciting. Yet
here he was, suddenly struggling to get air into his lungs. The shortness
of breath came on much faster this time than in the past.

"Viola, you better come down here," he managed to call out before
sitting down in an antique oak rocking chair in the family room.

His wife, an elderly woman with wisps of white hair that framed
her face, appeared almost instantly. "Red, what on earth is the matter?"
He had gotten his nickname many decades ago, back when he had
sported a full head of curly red hair. Now those locks were long gone;
they had been replaced with a shiny bald dome instead. "You were fine
just a few minutes ago."

"I can't seem to catch my breath. I think you better call for an ambulance. But remember, no medics."

Red was adamantly opposed to paramedics. Deep down he realized that they'd helped him quite a bit the first time he went to the hospital, but then he was hopping mad when he got their bill. In actuality, his insurance covered the entire cost. He hadn't paid a dime out of his own pocket. However, he insisted that it was the principle of the thing. The next two times the volunteer squad took him to the hospital, he refused the medics. The volunteers were upset and tried unsuccessfully to get him to change his mind. As far as he was concerned, it worked out okay in the end because he made it to the hospital before his breathing got really bad.

Viola was of the same mind as her husband. She had told him she didn't want the paramedics to come either. "I'll call right away, dear." She hustled to the phone in the kitchen.

. . . .

DISPATCHER: "Request for first aid at 672 Waverly Drive for a 91-year-old male with difficulty breathing."

As we headed out in the ambulance, Meg Potter wrote the address of the first aid call at the top of the run sheet. "We've been to this house before. It's the couple that always refuses the medics."

I pulled the first aid kit off its shelf. "Let's hope they feel differently now. He was in pretty bad respiratory distress last time."

Ted O'Malley cracked open a portable oxygen tank to check its pressure, knowing that we often needed more than one tank for this patient. "Congestive heart failure is tough. He said they can't operate on him."

"The house is on your left," Buddy Stone called to us from the driver's seat. "We're on location at 672 Waverly Drive," he told dispatch.

Officer McGovern met us at the front door. "They refused the medics again. Though honestly, he looks like he could really use them.

I already put him on oxygen." We followed him inside, through the living room and kitchen to a large family room with floor-to-ceiling windows.

"We don't want the medics," Viola said before we could even say hello.

"No medics," Red repeated. "Just get me to the hospital right away." His face looked pale, and perspiration gleamed above his upper lip.

"Sir, if you don't mind me saying so, the medics could really help you. They could provide advanced life support," Meg said.

"No thanks. I know all about them. I don't need them. I have the utmost confidence in you." Red paused after every two or three words to catch his breath.

"Thank you, but we strongly advise you to reconsider," Ted said.

"No. Let's move on," he replied stubbornly.

Sighing, I knelt next to Red to check his vital signs. "His blood pressure is 144 over 96. Heart rate 112. Respirations 26 and labored. Pulse ox is 92 percent on high-flow oxygen. Lung sounds are diminished bilaterally at the bases. It sounds like he has rales."

Red also had a bluish hue around his lips and nail beds. It was obvious that he wasn't getting enough air, even with the high-flow oxygen. *He looks much worse than last time. He looks like he could code or go into respiratory arrest at any minute.* "Code" is the term we use to indicate cardiac arrest. I fervently hoped we wouldn't be using that word aloud on this call.

"I have the past medical history and medications written down. We can load him onto the cot now," Meg said.

"You don't have to lift me. I can do it by myself," Red puffed.

Ted got on one side of Red, and I got on the other. We helped him stand up and pivot his feet so he could sit down on our stretcher. Even though we tried to limit his exertion as much as possible, I could see that it still took a toll on him.

"Is there any chance of you changing your mind about the medics?" I asked. "We could still call them."

"No chance. Let's go. I'll be fine," Red said firmly.

We used a four-person lift to carry the stretcher down the front porch steps and quickly loaded Red into our ambulance. "He looks terrible," Meg whispered to me. "I hope we make it there."

As soon as we got in the ambulance, I recounted his respirations. "I'm going to use something called a bag valve mask to help your breathing," I explained. "It might take a little bit of the work off you, okay?"

As I set up the BVM, pink, frothy sputum began bubbling out of Red's nose and spraying out of his mouth. Wordlessly, I put down the bag valve mask and began setting up the suction unit. After running the suction tubing through sterile water, I handed it to Meg.

Meg began suctioning some of the fluid away. "It's pulmonary edema." Pulmonary edema is an accumulation of fluid in the lungs. It can come on suddenly in patients with heart failure, leading to difficulty breathing. Heart failure is often caused by inadequate pumping of the left ventricle of the heart.

When Meg was finished suctioning, I placed the BVM over Red's nose and mouth and tried to coordinate my squeezing with his breathing efforts.

"Step it up," Ted called to Buddy, who was driving. "And ask the dispatcher to call ahead to the ER. Tell them we're coming, and we'll need help right away."

Red grabbed my hand and squeezed it hard. "I can't breathe," he gasped. We'd already sat up the back of the stretcher as far as it could go. We'd suctioned him and were helping him breathe. There was nothing left in our bag of tricks. If the medics were with us, they could have tried CPAP (continuous positive airway pressure) or may have intubated him. They would have initiated breathing treatments and administered other potentially life-saving medications. But, unfortunately, we didn't have the medics with us. We were on our own.

I breathed a sigh of relief when we pulled into the hospital's parking lot. As we hustled Red down the ER corridor, I prayed he would somehow manage to hold on.

Triage Nurse Maggie Summers met us at the door. "Straight to room 2," she directed us. Just as we rolled into room 2, Red's head slumped forward, and he stopped breathing. "We've got a code in room 2!" Maggie yelled. A team of nurses, a physician, and a respiratory therapist began working on Red right away.

Feeling decidedly unsettled, I stepped out of the room and pulled the curtain closed behind me. I knew that Viola was driving her car to the hospital and would be there any minute. I flinched when I thought of the terrible shock she would have when she saw how badly her husband's condition had deteriorated.

. . . .

Several days later, while I was working as a physical therapist, I paused at the threshold of Red's medical intensive care unit room. I breathed a sigh of relief; he was alert and looking around. He noticed me right away and motioned me to come in. I glanced back at the nurses' station and spotted his nurse, Dana. "Go right ahead. He could use some cheering up," she said.

I stepped in and smiled. "Glad to see you're doing better, Mr. Wakefield."

With great animation, he frowned and pointed to the tube coming out of his mouth. Although he was awake, he was still intubated and hooked up to a ventilator. Motioning me closer, he pointed repeatedly to his lips.

I wasn't sure what he wanted. "Are you thirsty? Do you want to know when you can get the tube out?"

Frustrated, Red shook his head and pointed to his lips again. "Are your lips dry? Your tongue dry?" He shook his head vehemently. "Okay, I'll let your nurse know," I said, even though I still didn't understand what he was trying to tell me. I felt bad that he appeared so uncomfortable. Unfortunately, there's nothing comfortable about having a tube down your throat. I chatted for a few minutes to try to take his mind off his troubles. *Hopefully he'll be off the ventilator and home again within a few weeks.*

. . . .

Four months later

A sinking feeling welled up in the pit of Red's stomach. Pausing in the middle of balancing his checkbook, he slowly put his pen down and closed his eyes. He sat at his desk in denial for several minutes, but eventually he had to admit that it was getting harder and harder to breathe. The shortness of breath felt just like his previous episodes of congestive heart failure, which came on quickly and with little warning.

"Honey," he called out, hoping Viola was within earshot.

"Yes, dear. Do you need something?"

He wanted to shout, but his words came out more like a hoarse whisper. "Come here, please."

A few seconds later, Viola popped her head into the office. She took one look at him and said, "I'll call for the ambulance."

A frown creased Red's brow. "No medics."

"Of course not, Red. I'll tell the dispatcher that we don't want them."

. . . .

DISPATCHER: "Request for first aid at 672 Waverly Drive for a 91-year-old male with shortness of breath."

Once again, Officer McGovern met us at the front door. "His wife told our dispatcher not to call for the medics, but he dispatched them anyway. When I got here, he and his wife said they didn't want them. I explained that they were already on their way here, and it looked like he could really benefit from them, but they made me cancel them," he said apologetically.

"Thanks," I said. "I'm going to give it my best shot to change his mind." Ted, Buddy, and I passed through the living room and turned right into a small office. Red sat perched on the edge of his chair, struggling to breathe. The veins on the sides of his neck bulged out, signaling his respiratory distress.

I knelt next to him and looked him straight in the eye. "Please, Mr. Wakefield, I need you to reconsider. I want the paramedics to help you."

"No medics," he said weakly.

Viola stood in the doorway. "No medics. We don't need them. You got him to the hospital just fine last time."

"Mr. Wakefield, not to be blunt, but we did not get you to the hospital 'just fine' last time. We barely made it there, and you stopped breathing just as we arrived. We all know how bad you get and how quickly it happens."

He shook his head no, but I persisted. "Do you realize how serious this is? You look like you need the breathing tube again. We can't do that for you. We need the medics for that."

"No medics," Viola repeated. "Just get him in the ambulance."

"Please. I wouldn't ask you if I thought we could get you there okay." In my mind, I could already picture him going into respiratory arrest. It wasn't a pretty picture.

"Okay," he whispered.

Relief rushed through me like a turbulent river. I turned toward Officer McGovern. "Please call back the medics right away."

"We don't want the medics," Viola protested. "Don't call."

"Sorry, it's not up to you. It's up to your husband. And we're calling them right now."

Pink, frothy sputum started leaking from Red's mouth and nose. As I suctioned the sputum away, Buddy hurriedly took a set of vital signs. Then we lifted Red onto our stretcher.

"Remember last time when I squeezed the bag with the mask to help you breathe?" I asked.

Red nodded his head ever so slightly.

"I'm going to do that again, okay?" I immediately began squeezing the BVM, once again timing my efforts to match his. Fortunately, the medics weren't too far away when we re-dispatched them. By the time we loaded Red into the rig, Rose Anderson and William Moore pulled up behind us in their ambulance. I don't think I've ever been so relieved to see them as I was at that minute.

William took one glance at Red before asking him, "Have you ever had a breathing tube before?" Red nodded, so William asked, "Do I have your permission to put one in right now?"

Once again, Red nodded.

I'm so relieved he changed his mind about the paramedics. He surely would have gone into respiratory arrest and possibly cardiac arrest in the back of our ambulance. Now he has a better chance of surviving.

I suctioned a little more fluid from Red's mouth, and then William sedated and intubated him. Rose established intravenous access and applied a 12-lead ECG. After that, it was a relatively peaceful trip to the hospital. Ted squeezed the BVM once every five seconds, and the medics monitored Red's condition.

About ten minutes later, we pulled into the Bakersville Hospital emergency department parking lot. Maggie Summers ushered us directly into room 3, where emergency room physician Dr. Parnell was waiting for us. After we transferred Red from our stretcher to the hospital's, I slowly stepped out of the room and pulled the curtain closed behind me.

. . . .

You...have received the law that was given through angels but have not obeyed it.

ACTS 7:53

Sometimes God is trying to help us, but for whatever reason, we resist. We are provided with a solution to our problem, but we shrug it off. I was grateful that Red eventually agreed to allow the paramedics to help him. After spending ten days on a ventilator in the intensive care unit, Red recovered and was able go home. He lived for several more years, and he didn't have to go back on a ventilator again.

21

Getting into Hot Water

Have mercy on me, my God, have mercy on me,
for in you I take refuge.
I will take refuge in the shadow of your wings
until the disaster has passed.

PSALM 57:1

Karen Black inhaled deeply as she rode her bike, savoring the way the fresh spring air ruffled her hair and tickled her nose. Rays of early morning sunshine danced across Weeping Willow Lake, sparkling like exotic jewels. Karen loved cycling, though she was a late bloomer. She'd only learned how to ride a bicycle when she turned 50. Yesterday, on her sixtieth birthday, her husband had replaced her old-fashioned beach cruiser with a state-of-the-art, 21-speed mountain bike. Although she had taken it out for a brief spin around the block yesterday, today was her first official ride.

Karen veered off the sidewalk and headed across the thick green grass toward the lake. As she cruised down the grassy embankment, she picked up speed. Low-hanging branches of a pine tree stroked her arm with their needles as she whizzed by, almost as if to voice their approval of her flight.

Accustomed to her old beach cruiser, Karen pushed back with her right foot to activate the brakes. When she failed to slow down, she pushed back harder, but her pedals kept spinning backward.

Desperately, she tried to squeeze the hand brake levers, but it was too late. Like the songbirds soaring above her, Karen's bike had taken flight, sailing full speed into the lake.

. . . .

DISPATCHER: "Request for first aid at Weeping Willow Lake for a cyclist in the water."

I hopped into the driver's seat of the ambulance, and Meg Potter slipped into the passenger seat next to me. "Let's go," she murmured as she buckled her seat belt. "I can't even imagine how this could have happened."

"I'm not sure. Maybe it's a child," I suggested.

We arrived at the lake just in time to see Sergeant Flint standing in shallow lake water, giving a helping hand to a middle-aged woman as he guided her out of the lake. "This is Karen Black," he called back to us. "She lost control of her bike."

"I'm so embarrassed. I'm fine, really. Please just take me down to the beach and let me bury my head in the sand," Karen said.

"No worries. Everyone has accidents. That's why they call them that," Meg said.

"You have a nasty gash on your leg," I pointed out. "For starters, let's clean that up and put a bandage on it."

"I guess that's a good idea. My husband gave me the bike yesterday for my birthday. You should have seen how beautiful it looked with a big red bow tied onto the handlebars. How am I going to explain that it's in the lake?"

"You won't have to," Sergeant Flint replied. He waded a few feet back into the lake, grabbed her bicycle by the handlebars and frame, and hoisted it onto the grass. Unfortunately, the new bike was now coated with a fresh layer of greenish-brown slime.

Karen sat on a nearby bench. "Thank you so much. I'm just sorry that it got so muddy. It sure doesn't look brand-new anymore. Yesterday, it was absolutely sparkling."

"It's okay. We can take care of that," Meg said. After we bandaged Karen's leg, we used a bottle of sterile water and a few of our first aid towels to give her bike a thorough wiping down.

"Good as new. Your husband will never even know," I proclaimed.

"I'm going to drop off your bike at your home, if that's okay with you. I can leave it right by your garage," Sergeant Flint said.

"That would be perfect. Thank you all so much."

Meg and I transported Karen to the emergency room to get her wound examined and receive a tetanus shot. I hoped she'd be back to riding her bike again within a few days.

. . . .

The hot summer sun blazed brightly in the azure sky, obscured only infrequently by puffy cumulus clouds. Slim McWinters tapped the edge of the public pool with his right hand and pushed off to begin his next lap. *Eighteen laps down, eighteen to go.* Rain or shine, Slim swam a half mile every day. Of course, like most people, he preferred shine.

Slim was a big believer in staying physically fit and eating healthy. He started each morning with a well-balanced breakfast of whole grain cereal with almond milk, five prunes, and a banana. After his morning swim, he would enjoy a lunch of tuna salad on whole-grain toast, a handful of nuts, and an orange. Dinner would be something equally healthy, like salmon, brown rice, broccoli, and a side salad. He loved reading medical journals and health magazines to keep abreast of the latest nutrition research.

Slim hadn't always been a fitness nut. He had changed his ways after his father suffered a fatal heart attack and his brother needed open-heart surgery.

Slim paused at the end of the pool lane to rest a moment, which was something he normally didn't have to do. His legs felt oddly heavy, and he couldn't catch his breath. He decided to keep swimming and drink a bottle of water when he was done.

Once again, he pushed off the wall and began swimming the breast-stroke. Suddenly, the other end of the pool appeared far away. Almost out of the blue, he felt as though a hippopotamus had somehow jumped into the pool and was now sitting on his chest. *Ten more strokes. Surely, I can make it ten more strokes.* But all at once, he wasn't sure if he could. *Should I do something to attract the lifeguard's attention?*

Slim somehow found himself in the shallow end of the pool. Managing to get his feet on the bottom, he staggered toward the pool's entry steps. An alert lifeguard, concerned that Slim hadn't finished his lap as strongly as he usually did, rushed to the stairs to see if everything was okay.

"Call 911. I'm having a heart attack." Slim collapsed at the edge of the pool.

. . . .

DISPATCHER: "Request for first aid at the town pool for a man having a heart attack. Patient is unconscious at this time."

Alec Waters flipped on the ambulance's lights and sirens. "We're responding. Do you have a patient update for us?"

"Patient is now alert and conscious, complaining of crushing chest pain and difficulty breathing," Dispatcher Franklin responded.

Alec, Colleen Harper, and I rushed along the boardwalk into the pool area. A small crowd surrounded an older gentleman, who was sitting on a woven plastic folding chair. A young woman with long braided hair was holding a large beach umbrella over him to provide some shade. The man was soaking wet, though it appeared at least some of it was due to perspiration and not just residual pool water. His face appeared unnaturally white with grayish undertones. From a glance, he looked like a gravely ill man.

Officer Endicott looked up from tending to the gentleman. "This is Slim McWinters. He suddenly went into distress while swimming laps. The lifeguard estimates that he passed out for about sixty seconds. He's now complaining of severe, crushing mid-sternal chest pain radiating to the left arm and difficulty breathing. I've just gotten him on oxygen."

"Mr. McWinters, do you carry nitro pills with you?" Alec asked.

Slim shook his head. "I don't take any medications. I do have a family history of cardiac problems though."

"Blood pressure is 92 over 60. Pulse is 104 and strong. Respirations are 18. Lungs clear," Colleen rattled off. "Negative JVD, negative pedal edema." JVD, a bulging of the external jugular veins at the sides of the neck, stands for jugular venous distension. If a person has significant JVD while their head is elevated more than 45 degrees, it can indicate heart or vascular disease. Pedal edema refers to swelling of the feet and ankles. When the heart weakens and pumps less effectively, pedal edema can develop.

We lifted Slim onto our stretcher and wheeled him a short distance to our ambulance, eager to get him out of the sun and on the way to the hospital. "I feel terrible. I've worried that this day might come, and yet I can't believe this is really happening to me."

I gently patted his shoulder to console him. I knew his symptoms must be terrifying him.

About a half mile from the pool, we pulled over to meet up with medics Arthur Williamson and Kennisha Smythe. Arthur quickly applied a 12-lead ECG. After studying the ECG tracing for a moment, he said, "It looks like an acute MI." Kennisha gained IV access and took blood samples so the hospital's lab could perform cardiac enzyme testing. Positive results would indicate that Slim was indeed suffering a myocardial infarction (MI).

Although his blood pressure was too low to administer nitroglycerin, he could chew on a baby aspirin. It was easy to see that his condition was quite unstable. He would most likely need a cardiac catheterization to examine his coronary blood vessels for blockages. The next few hours would prove critical in determining his outcome.

"Straight to room 4," Maggie directed when we arrived in the triage area. "We'll need to prep him for the cath lab."

An emergency room technician helped us slide Slim from our stretcher to the hospital's. We knew it was important that he not exert himself.

I adjusted the pillow under Slim's head. "I'll be thinking of you," I said.

Slim nodded. "Thank you. But please do more than think of me. Pray for me."

"Of course," I said, giving his hand a quick squeeze.

. . . .

At Caesarea there was a man named Cornelius, a centurion in what was known as the Italian Regiment. He and all his family were devout and God-fearing; he gave generously to those in need and prayed to God regularly. One day at about three in the afternoon he had a vision. He distinctly saw an angel of God, who came to him and said, "Cornelius!"

Cornelius stared at him in fear. "What is it, Lord?" he asked.

The angel answered, "Your prayers and gifts to the poor have come up as a memorial offering before God. Now send men to Joppa to bring back a man named Simon who is called Peter. He is staying with Simon the tanner, whose house is by the sea."

When the angel who spoke to him had gone, Cornelius called two of his servants and a devout soldier who was one of his attendants. He told them everything that had happened and sent them to Joppa.

ACTS 10:1-8

Slim, a Christian, requested our prayers when we left him in the emergency room. The Bible shows us that God hears our prayers. He may send angels to intercede as our protectors, helping to carry us through life's storms. Our squad learned that Slim received two emergency cardiac stents that day and went on to make a full recovery.

22

Where's the Call?

I trust in you, Lord;
I say, "You are my God."

PSALM 31:14

Taylor Hendrickson and her husband, Zeke, had planned this weekend getaway to Pine Cove for months. It would be their last vacation as a couple; the next one would be as a family.

Now 32 weeks pregnant, it was getting harder and harder for Taylor to sleep comfortably. Although it was the middle of the night, she lay awake, thinking how blessed she was to finally have a baby inside her. It hadn't been an easy road for Zeke and her. They had struggled with infertility for years. During that difficult time, she had suffered several devastating miscarriages. She didn't like to dwell on those sad days. Absentmindedly, she rubbed her abdomen.

Taylor shifted in bed and suddenly became aware of a strange, sticky sensation between her legs. Paralyzed with fear, she almost couldn't bring herself to get up and see what was wrong. But she knew that she'd have to act soon; she was the type of person who faced her troubles head-on. She threw back the covers, sat up on the edge of the bed, and switched on a small bedside lamp. It was just as she'd feared. Dark red blood stained her bedding. "Zeke, wake up," she said urgently.

Zeke propped himself up on his elbow. "What's wrong? Can't sleep?

Heartburn? Leg cramps? Do you need me to get you some antacid pills?"

Placing her head between her hands, Taylor began to weep. "Look at the bed," she managed to choke out between sobs.

Zeke took one glance and jumped to his feet. "I'll call for an ambulance right away."

. . . .

> **DISPATCHER:** "Request for first aid at 320 Meade Street for a woman with severe hemorrhaging."

When my pager went off, I sat bolt upright in my bed. *That's my address. That's our house. We have a first aid call at our house? Is Mom okay? I'm on the first aid squad. Wouldn't they wake me up first if something was wrong? Wouldn't they tell me before calling 911?* Baffled, I jumped out of bed and rushed to my parents' room. It was dark, and they were both sleeping soundly.

My mother, a light sleeper, roused when I stepped into the room. "What are you doing up at this hour?" she asked.

"My pager just went off and said we have a call right here."

My mother turned on her bedside lamp. "Here? For what?"

"A woman with severe hemorrhaging." I quickly dialed the local police department. "Hi, it's Andrea from the first aid squad. You just dispatched the squad for a first aid call at my address, but it's not here."

"Okay, thanks," Dispatcher Franklin said. "I'm not surprised; the caller stated that he was visiting the area and was uncertain as to exactly where they're staying. I'll get an accurate address." True to his word, by the time I reached the first aid building, he had already re-dispatched us with a corrected location.

After Jessie Barnes, Dillon Chapman, and I arrived at the scene of the first aid call with the ambulance, we entered the home through the rear entrance and began climbing a narrow flight of stairs toward the third floor.

Officer McGovern looked up as we entered the bedroom. "Taylor just stepped into the bathroom. If you look at the bed, you'll see that there's quite a bit of blood. She's thirty-two weeks pregnant with a history of two miscarriages."

I knocked gently on the bathroom door. "Taylor?" I thought I heard a muffled "yes," so I asked, "Can I come in?"

Her husband, a tall man with broad shoulders, pushed open the door. "Come in," he said gruffly. I could tell that he was trying to be strong for his wife but struggling to do so.

"Taylor, we need to take you to the hospital right away, okay?" After she nodded, I carefully led her toward our stair chair. "We don't want you to walk, so we're going to carry you downstairs."

"Please tell me my baby didn't die," she begged.

My heart grieved for her. In truth, none of us had any idea if she had already lost her baby or not, though it appeared to be a strong possibility. I wanted to comfort her, but at the same time, I didn't want to give her false hope.

"We're going to take you to the nearest hospital so the obstetrician can help you," I said. Dillon and Jessie strapped Taylor into the stair chair and carried her down to the first floor, where we met up with paramedics Rose Anderson and William Moore.

"We'll assess in the rig," Rose said, echoing my own thought process. I knew that for Taylor and Zeke's baby to have any chance of surviving, it would be better if Taylor were in the hospital. If she hadn't lost the baby yet, then trying to deliver an infant who was eight weeks premature would be terribly risky. Every minute counted.

Taylor continued to bleed all the way to the emergency room. There wasn't a whole lot we could do except monitor her condition.

"I can't take any more. We were so close this time. I just don't understand," Taylor said.

We left the couple in one of the triage rooms with heavy hearts. *With all that blood, it'll be a miracle if that child survives.*

. . . .

When they had gone, an angel of the Lord appeared to Joseph in a dream. "Get up," he said, "take the child and his mother and escape to Egypt. Stay there until I tell you, for Herod is going to search for the child to kill him."

So he got up, took the child and his mother during the night and left for Egypt, where he stayed until the death of Herod. And so was fulfilled what the Lord had said through the prophet: "Out of Egypt I called my son."

MATTHEW 2:13-15

Once again, we see in Scripture that angels appear in dreams to guide and protect. In Matthew 2, we learn that an angel appeared to Joseph in a dream in order to keep Jesus safe.

Young children tug at our heartstrings. First responders are truly blessed when they can assist infants and their families. Although Taylor's unborn baby appeared to be in grave danger, we learned one week later that Taylor gave birth to a healthy baby girl.

The Beat Goes On

With you is the fountain of life;
in your light we see light.

PSALM 36:9

Shivering, Barbara Charleston rolled to her side and tugged at her blankets. Somehow, her covers always seemed to slide down toward the bottom of the bed. Without even looking at the alarm clock, she knew it was almost time to get up. The baby monitor was quiet, so she decided to enjoy these last few minutes of rest before another busy day.

Baby Maribelle was turning exactly seven weeks old today, and Barbara reflected on what a joy she had been in her life. She and her husband, Hector, had tried for several years to conceive before they were blessed with their beautiful daughter. Although Barbara was fatigued, she was relishing every single minute of motherhood.

Barbara was used to hearing her daughter make adorable cooing noises or at least rustle about, and it concerned her that she hadn't heard anything from the nursery yet. As she stood up, she glanced over at Hector. He was snoring softly, obviously also feeling the effects of long days and short nights.

Throwing on a warm fleece robe, Barbara padded barefoot down the hall to the nursery. *Maribelle looks so pale.* Tentacles of unease wound themselves around Barbara's neck, pulling her closer to the crib.

"Good morning, sunshine," she said brightly, determined to counteract her anxiety that something could be wrong. *Why is she so still?*

Quickly lowering the crib rail, she gathered her daughter into her arms. Much to her horror, Maribelle flopped lifelessly like a rag doll. *Why is she so cold? What's wrong with her?* "Maribelle!" she cried out, giving her a little shake. Full-blown terror now consumed her. Rushing down the hall with Maribelle in her arms, she screamed, "Hector, wake up. Something's wrong with the baby!"

Roused from a deep sleep, Hector jumped to his feet, his expression a mix of confusion and fear. "What's wrong? Is she sick?"

"I don't think she's breathing. Call for an ambulance!"

. . . .

DISPATCHER: "Request for first aid at 39 Crestview Drive for a report of an infant not breathing."

No way. It must be a mistake. Surely the baby is breathing. Nevertheless, I hustled into my car and hurried toward Crestview Drive. *Maybe the baby turned blue or briefly stopped breathing after a febrile seizure.* We often respond to first aid calls for infants who have a seizure due to fever.

A few seconds later my pager was activated again, and the dispatcher's words directly contradicted my thoughts.

DISPATCHER: "Update on the call at 39 Crestview Drive. As per patrol on scene, expedite. CPR is in progress."

I felt my heart suddenly sink down toward my toes, while at the same time a rush of horror-induced adrenaline surged through me. *I've practiced CPR on infant mannequins dozens of times, but I've never done it on a real baby. Babies are not supposed to die.*

When I arrived, I slammed my car into park and started running toward house number 39. I was dimly aware that fellow squad member

Helen McGuire was also pulling up to the scene, wearing an equally stunned expression. Wordlessly, with matching strides, we rushed down the driveway, up the porch steps, and into the home. Hearing noises upstairs, we followed the sounds to the second floor.

I can't believe this is happening. But as I entered the bedroom, I was forced to accept that it was true. Officer Kyle Jamieson knelt on the bedroom floor, performing CPR on a tiny baby girl. Incredibly brave and smart, Officer Jamieson was a shining example of one of our town's "men in blue." His skills were now being put to a task that none of us had previously encountered.

My gaze caught sight of the tiny bag valve mask, and I suppressed a small shiver.

"Her mother found her unresponsive in the crib. The exact down time is unknown, but when I got here, she felt somewhat cool to the touch. I started CPR right away," Officer Jamieson said.

The infant's mother sat hunched over on the edge of her bed, her head cradled in her hands and her long red hair covering her face. Gut-wrenching sobs racked her body, and her shoulders shook uncontrollably. On the other side of the room stood a distraught man who I figured must be the baby's father. His expression was one of absolute shock, as though he had stepped into the worst nightmare of his life. The parents' bone-numbing grief was almost palpable. I tried to block it out. I knew we had a job to do. *Focus on the baby. Do your job. And pray.*

"The rig's pulling up now. There's a three-minute ETA on the paramedics," Helen said.

A moment later, Jessie Barnes and Kerry Branson rushed into the room. Kerry, a busy architect, still somehow found time to volunteer with our squad. "I saw the medics pulling up as we came in," she said.

Sensitive to the parents' feelings, Helen quietly filled Jessie and Kerry in on what she had learned. "She's seven weeks old. Her name is Maribelle," I heard her whisper.

I pulled the smallest oral airway out of our kit and held it up to the baby's face. As small as it was, it still looked big compared to her tiny face.

Helen passed me the suction unit. "Maybe you should get this ready, just in case. I'm going to try to get the rest of the history from the mother."

Mentally, I couldn't help but do the math. Maribelle's chances looked grim at best. The pallor of death clung to her. *Fight, Maribelle. Hang in there, baby girl.*

Kerry assisted Officer Jamieson with CPR. With so many of us crowded around the tiny infant, we were literally all shoulder to shoulder. When medics Rose Anderson and William Moore entered the room, I eased out of the way to give them some space.

The following minutes passed in a hazy blur of emergency medicine at its saddest. The sounds of the mother's unrelenting sobs filled the air. "Is she dead?" I kept hearing her ask in between her sobs. "Is she going to die? Please, someone tell me she isn't going to die."

William placed electrodes on Baby Maribelle's chest, arms, and legs and hooked her up to their heart monitor. "She's in a nonshockable rhythm. Continue CPR," he said, meaning we could not use the defibrillator to revive her.

My hopes for a successful outcome dropped one notch further at his words. I sneaked another glance at Maribelle's father. He wore the same exact look of astonished denial that he wore when we had first entered the room.

Rose established an IV line for Maribelle and pushed through several medications designed to help resuscitate her. *Will they work? At this point, it's been so long…*

Meanwhile, William inserted the smallest endotracheal tube I have even seen into Maribelle's airway. Kerry detached the mask from the BVM, and William then hooked it up to the end of the endotracheal tube. "Okay, give the bag gentle squeezes," he said.

Several minutes passed as our team worked feverishly to resuscitate Maribelle.

"Hold CPR for a second. I think I might see something on the monitor," Rose said.

Officer Jamieson leaned back on his heels, lifting his hand away from Maribelle's chest.

Rose placed two fingers on Maribelle's left brachial artery. "I have a brachial pulse. William, can you confirm that on her right arm?"

"I feel it too. It's actually quite strong. Let's just continue with the rescue breathing," he said.

I'm not sure if getting her pulse back is good or bad. After all this time, it would be almost impossible for Maribelle not to have brain damage. I exchanged a quick look with Helen and wondered if she was thinking the same thing.

While we prepared Maribelle for transport to the hospital, her little heart kept beating. However, her color remained poor and she made no effort to breathe on her own. I tried to stifle the feeling that this call was going to have a bad outcome. Amid the sounds of the mother's sobs, we carried her beloved daughter out to the ambulance.

· · · · · · · · · · · · ·

"Maribelle's brain dead and on life support," William told us the next evening while we were on a first aid call for a middle-aged gentleman complaining of chest pains.

Brain dead. On life support. The words slowly sank in, even though I didn't want to hear them. I honestly hadn't thought that Baby Maribelle would make it through the night. Now it seemed like her parents' heartbreak was destined to continue, at least for the time being.

"Any chance at all? Could there be a mistake?" Helen asked.

William shook his head. "No, I'm afraid not. Such a sad business."

"It's the kind of call that will stick with us forever," Jessie said.

I nodded in agreement. "Forever and then some." I knew the memories would fade with time, but for now they seemed determined to remain front and center in my consciousness.

"Poor little girl is clinging on. Just remember, you all did a great job yesterday. You did what you're trained to do," Rose said.

I appreciated her words of comfort as I tried to make sense of the tragedy. We had all worked so hard to bring back Maribelle's heartbeat, but to what end?

· · · · · · · · · · · · ·

Days passed. Baby Maribelle and her family were never very far from my mind. I wondered how Barbara and Hector would be able to find the strength to let go of Maribelle and say goodbye.

While Jessie, Helen, and I were dropping off a patient in the emergency room, we ran into Rose and William in the hallway. "Any news?" Helen asked. She didn't have to specify news about what. We all knew she was asking about Baby Maribelle.

"Actually, yes," Rose said solemnly.

I braced myself. I knew deep down there could be no miraculous recovery for Maribelle. And yet, I wasn't sure if I was ready to hear that she was truly gone. Even so, Rose's next words caught me by surprise.

"Maribelle's parents decided to donate her heart. So, although she's gone, her heart is now beating in the chest of another baby halfway across the country."

Rose's words slowly penetrated, lifting some of the gloom I had carried with me the past few days. *Baby Maribelle's life wasn't in vain. We didn't bring back her heartbeat for nothing after all. Because of her, another baby lives.*

I reflected that the anguish of one family became the salvation of another. If not for the gift of Baby Maribelle's heart, two lives could have been lost instead of one. I appreciated the Charleston family's selfless gift in such a time of devastation and despair. It made all our hope and effort worth it, and it helped lift at least a small measure of the sadness that shrouded my memories of that day. I pictured Baby Maribelle's heart beating strongly, sustaining the life of another infant many miles away. *The beat goes on.*

• • • • • • • • • • • • •

Years later, I was browsing in the public library when my attention was drawn by a small voice that said, "Look at this one, Mommy." Sitting on a cozy love seat was Barbara Charleston and an adorable little girl with wavy brown hair.

I quickly edged back behind a shelf of books, as I didn't want Barbara to see me. I wasn't sure if she would even recognize me, but if she did, I knew that my face might be tied to unhappy memories. I didn't want to take that risk.

The little girl let out a squeal of excitement, pointing with great animation to one of the pages in the book that rested on her mother's lap. When I witnessed the sight of Barbara smiling brightly, leaning over the book with her young daughter, my heart quietly let go of some of the residual pain I had held on to all these years—and with that release came acceptance.

. . . .

An angel of the Lord appeared to [Zechariah], standing at the right side of the altar of incense. When Zechariah saw him, he was startled and was gripped with fear. But the angel said to him: "Do not be afraid, Zechariah; your prayer has been heard. Your wife Elizabeth will bear you a son, and you are to call him John. He will be a joy and delight to you, and many will rejoice because of his birth, for he will be great in the sight of the Lord. He is never to take wine or other fermented drink, and he will be filled with the Holy Spirit even before he is born. He will bring back many of the people of Israel to the Lord their God. And he will go on before the Lord, in the spirit and power of Elijah, to turn the hearts of the parents to their children and the disobedient to the wisdom of the righteous—to make ready a people prepared for the Lord."

LUKE 1:11-17

The plight of Baby Maribelle reminded me of the passage above. The first chapter of Luke gives hope to infertile couples. I tried to make sense of Maribelle's death by taking some measure of comfort in the fact that another baby survived because of the gift of her heart. Although Maribelle could never be replaced, I was glad her parents were able to have another child. I hoped it would ease some of their pain at the loss of their daughter.

Matthew tells us that each of our little ones has an angel watching over them:

See that you do not despise one of these little ones. For I tell you that their angels in heaven always see the face of my Father in heaven.

MATTHEW 18:10

24

Falling off the Wagon

My heart is in anguish within me;
the terrors of death have fallen on me.
Fear and trembling have beset me;
horror has overwhelmed me.
I said, "Oh, that I had the wings of a dove!
I would fly away and be at rest."

PSALM 55:4-6

Jeff Martins pulled his taxicab over and parked in front of Pine Cove Apartments. He knew exactly where his passenger lived, which was good because she often passed out on the way there. He'd been driving Sugar Humphrey home from various local bars at least once a week for the past year or two. Whenever she called for a cab, no matter how intoxicated she was, she always somehow managed to request him by name. He didn't mind driving her, except that she sometimes vomited. The first time, it got all over the seat and floor of his cab. After that, he wised up and kept disposable bags on hand. Usually, Sugar was just sober enough that she could use the bag without spilling.

"Ms. Humphrey, it's time to wake up. We're here," he said.

"Thank you," she replied, slurring her words slightly. "What do I owe you?"

"Eight dollars would be fine, thanks."

She fished a ten-dollar bill out of her purse and handed it to him. "Keep the change. Thanks again."

"I'll wait here until I see you get safely inside." Jeff made it a habit of doing so because he worried that she might trip and fall before she made it into her condo. Tonight, when one of her friends had walked her from the bar entrance out to his cab, she didn't look very steady on her feet.

Sometimes, Jeff was tempted to walk Sugar to her front door, but then he decided not to because he was afraid of the liability. Because she was always intoxicated, he was nervous she might lose her balance. Then if he grabbed her to steady her, she could accuse him of touching her inappropriately. No, sir. He didn't want to go down that road. He needed this job, and if something like that happened, his wife would have an absolute fit.

He watched as Sugar slowly made her way down the long sidewalk toward her front door, teetering on her high-heeled sandals. Just when he thought she was going to make it, she tripped and fell flat on her face.

Jeff jumped out of the car, rushed to her, and tapped her shoulder. "Ms. Humphrey, are you okay?"

She sounded like she was snoring, as though she had already fallen asleep. Gently, he pushed her onto her side so he could see her face. Blood oozed from her nose and mouth. She obviously hadn't put out her hands to break her fall.

He hurried back to his taxi and radioed his dispatch center. "My passenger fell in front of her apartment. Could you please send for an ambulance?"

．．．．．．．．．．．．．．

DISPATCHER: "Request for first aid at Pine Cove Apartments outside building 3 for an intoxicated female fall victim with facial injuries."

"I'll drive," Dillon Chapman said. "I think we've had this person before."

"I'm pretty sure I've been on a call for her, too, if she's the middle-aged woman with the platinum-blonde hair," Mason Chapman replied.

If it was the person we were thinking of, we'd picked her up once for severe intoxication and once for dehydration. I grabbed an emesis (vomit) basin to be on the safe side.

As we approached Pine Cove Apartments, a man who looked to be in his forties waved at us and pointed toward building 3. Once we'd parked and stepped out of the ambulance, he told us, "It's Ms. Humphrey. I think she drank too much. I'm not sure if she passed out and fell or if she tripped and lost her balance and then fell."

"Thank you for the information," I replied as we headed together toward building 3.

Officer Sims met us halfway. "She has a bloody nose. It looks like she may have knocked a tooth loose as well."

I started filling out our call sheet while Dillon and Mason attended to Sugar. I remembered she had a past medical history of hypertension and alcohol abuse and she was allergic to penicillin, but I couldn't recall the names of her medications. Sugar roused when we rolled her onto a backboard, at which point she promptly vomited. "Well, hopefully it's all out now," I said, relieved that Mason had placed the basin in front of her mouth just in time.

Sugar became more alert on the way to the hospital. "Why does my face feel funny? Did I fall?"

Mason wiped some dried blood off her forehead and cheeks with gauze and sterile water. "Yes, you fell and got a bloody nose. It's not bleeding anymore, but please try not to touch it."

She reached up with her left hand to touch her face despite Mason's warning. "Did I trip?"

"I'm not sure, but your cab driver thought you either passed out or tripped and lost your balance," I said. When Mason was done cleaning her up, I placed a cold pack over her nose and forehead.

"Can you come closer, so I can tell you a secret?" she asked. She tried to turn toward me, but the backboard straps prevented her.

"Sure," I said, leaning in but ready to move away quickly if she started vomiting again.

"Sometimes I drink a bit too much. But tonight, I only had two beers."

It's funny, but people often say they had "two beers," even when it's obvious they had quite a few more. We leave it up to the emergency department to determine exactly how much liquor a person has truly consumed.

When we arrived at the hospital, we gave the patient report to Maggie Summers, the triage nurse, and then headed home. I was looking forward to returning to the comfort of my bed for a few more hours.

· · · · · · · · · · · · ·

Several months later

As soon as Sugar was sure her sister had pulled out of the parking lot of the apartment complex, she began searching every cabinet for liquor. *Nothing. They must have hidden it or gotten rid of it.* Tears of frustration stung her eyes as she pounded her fist on the counter. Suddenly recalling where she'd hidden a stash of liquor, Sugar rushed to the small closet next to her bathroom and frantically rifled through a pile of fluffy blue bath towels on the second shelf. She reached her arm into the back corner and came up empty. *I don't believe it. They must have found that too.*

Desperation seized her, filling her with such a longing for beer that she scarcely knew what to do. *Let me search the closet once more.* Shelf by shelf, she carefully looked for a bottle of beer or wine that her family might have missed. Suddenly, her attention was drawn to one bottle in particular. *Well, it's going to taste terrible, but it'll have to do.*

· · · · · · · · · · · · ·

DISPATCHER: "Request for first aid at Pine Cove Apartments, building 3, apartment C, for an unresponsive female."

"I heard through the grapevine that Sugar just got home from rehab," Mason said.

"I hope she hasn't relapsed already," I replied.

The heavy wooden door to Sugar's apartment stood slightly ajar, so Mason tapped briefly as we entered. We passed through a living room cluttered with bric-a-brac and headed toward the rear of the apartment. Sugar lay propped up on several pillows on the right side of her queen-size bed. She looked extremely pale, and her breathing sounded labored, like each breath took an extreme amount of effort on her part.

A gentleman bearing a strong resemblance to Sugar looked up as we entered the bedroom. "I'm Sugar's brother, Melvin," he said, reaching out to shake our hands. "She just got out of rehab last week. We've had friends and family staying with her around the clock to make sure she doesn't fall off the wagon. We removed every single bit of alcohol from the apartment before she got home. I swear there wasn't a drop of beer, wine, or anything else in here. We had a one-hour gap today in watching her because my sister had to leave for an emergency with one of her kids. I got here as fast as I could. When I arrived, Sugar said that her stomach hurt and she felt dizzy."

Dillon felt Sugar's pulse at her wrist. "Did she say how long she had felt like that?"

"No, but my sister said Sugar was fine when she left an hour ago," Melvin said. "While I was with her, she seemed like she was getting confused, and her breathing started to sound funny. I helped her into bed and called 911 right away. I can't imagine what's wrong with her."

Officer Sims appeared in the bedroom holding a bottle of isopropyl alcohol in his hand. "I think I might have the answer. I found this uncapped on the bathroom counter."

Melvin looked both surprised and confused. "It never ever even occurred to me to remove something like that from her apartment. Is it very dangerous to drink that?"

"Unfortunately, denatured alcohol is extremely dangerous, even in small dosages," Mason replied. "It's poisonous when it's ingested. We're going to transport her to the emergency room right away."

"I just heard from dispatch that there's a three-minute ETA on the medics," Officer Sims said.

"Her blood pressure is low—86 over 40," Dillon said. After he finished assessing Sugar, we rolled her onto our Reeves (flexible stretcher) so that we could carry her around the tight hallway corners and onto our stretcher in the living room.

After we positioned her on our cot, I rechecked Sugar's pulse ox. "It's only 90 percent, despite being on high-flow oxygen."

"She's still completely unresponsive to stimuli," Mason said, just as medics Ty Fleming and Paula Pritchard entered the apartment. They efficiently established an IV line and secured Sugar's airway. Unfortunately, there wasn't a whole lot more any of us could do except transport her to the hospital.

We loaded Sugar into the ambulance. "She's probably going to get worse before she gets any better. If she gets any better," Paula said.

As I gazed at Sugar's face, it saddened me that she had gone to such lengths to consume alcohol, and now it could end her life. Almost as if reading my thoughts, Ty said, "This type of alcohol poisoning can be extremely lethal. Her odds for making it aren't very good at all, based on her current presentation." I was glad Melvin was sitting up front and couldn't hear Ty's dismal pronouncement.

Sugar remained unresponsive during the rest of the trip to the hospital. I felt terrible for her family. They had tried so hard to help her, yet somehow, she was on her way to the emergency room once again. And from the sound of it, she wouldn't be leaving anytime soon, if at all.

. . . .

He was in the wilderness forty days, being tempted by Satan. He was with the wild animals, and angels attended him.

MARK 1:13

Sugar spent several weeks in a coma in the medical intensive care unit. Ever so gradually, she regained consciousness and recovered from her near-lethal overdose. After being discharged from the hospital, she returned to rehab. I hoped this frightening episode would provide her with the incentive to turn away from alcohol once and for all. I prayed that with the loving support of her family and friends, and with God's angels attending her, she'd be able to stay on the wagon for good.

25

Flying High

As for me, I am poor and needy;
may the Lord think of me.
You are my help and my deliverer;
you are my God, do not delay.

PSALM 40:17

The big day—the day I had been looking forward to for countless months—was finally here. Today I'd be riding as an observer with a helicopter rescue unit. Knowing my passion for first aid, my brother had arranged this unique opportunity for me. I woke up at the crack of dawn and traveled several hours to the helicopter rescue headquarters nestled among city skyscrapers.

A middle-aged woman with bright blue eyes and a warm smile welcomed me when I arrived. "I'm Maeve. We're glad to have you riding with our team today. Your pilot will be Emmett, and your flight nurses are Julia and Lamont. They'll be arriving shortly. If you like, you can help yourself to a cup of coffee."

"Thank you so much. I'm excited that you're willing to let me tag along." As we made some small talk, I soaked in the ambience. The office wasn't particularly large, probably because the people who worked here spent most of their time up in the air. Maeve sat behind an L-shaped honey-oak desk, and a very large Boston fern hung from the ceiling in the corner behind her. Photos of helicopter rescue calls decorated the walls. A cozy floral love seat provided an additional colorful touch. The room blended comfort and efficiency.

As Maeve predicted, a trio of employees arrived a couple minutes later. A middle-aged gentleman with a trim physique held out his hand. "I heard we'd be having a ride-along today. I'm Emmett, and I'll be your pilot."

"And I'm one of the flight nurses, Julia," a petite woman with a gorgeous auburn braided bun said. "Nice to have you along."

A tall man with a thick head of brownish-gray curly hair smiled. "Hi, I'm Lamont. I hope we can arrange some action for you today."

"You have a terrific crew to observe," Maeve said. "And it looks as though you're going to have wonderful weather to boot. A bit breezy, but clear and sunny."

"I need to weigh you so I can make a few calculations," Emmett chimed in. "Please follow me." After I stepped onto a physician's scale, he jotted down my weight in a small notebook. "Sometimes it can be quiet the entire shift. I hope we can get the bird up into the sky for you."

I couldn't imagine coming all the way here and not having a single call. I had assumed the rescue team was constantly busy.

Almost as if by magic, my wish for some action came true a few minutes later, when Maeve called us back into the front room. "Time for you to head out. The call is for an interhospital cardiac transfer for a 72-year-old male."

"It's a nonemergency transport," Julia explained as we headed up to the roof, where the helicopter was kept. "Most likely, the patient needs to go from a small community hospital to a larger hospital to get the services he needs."

"Yes, for example, the patient may need some sort of emergency heart procedure," Lamont added.

As we stepped onto the roof, my eyes caught sight of a gleaming black helicopter with a white "Star of Life" emblem emblazoned on its side. *I can't believe I'm really getting this chance-of-a-lifetime opportunity.*

We climbed aboard, and Julia pointed to a small side seat. "Here's your spot. It's about a thirty-minute trip." Next, she helped me to put on a set of headphones. Then we were in the sky, and I was so excited, I had to remind myself to breathe. Soon we were flying above the buildings and treetops.

I settled in and wondered what our patient would be like. I hoped today would be a wonderful adventure.

· · · · · · · · · · · · · ·

Kirk Lyndon was married with two young children. He'd been unemployed for the past six months, so when his cousin got him a lead on a job as a window cleaner, he jumped at the opportunity. Now, as his scaffold swung disconcertingly in the wind, he was starting to question whether this job was the right fit for him.

He'd never been a huge fan of heights (he didn't even like flying in airplanes), but this was even worse than he'd anticipated. He glanced down, felt decidedly queasy, and refocused on the large window in front of him. He was only three floors up, but with the way the scaffold was shaking, if felt much higher to him. He was glad there was another guy up here with him, even if he didn't speak much. It was better than being alone.

Kirk glanced at his watch. "Almost break time," he said. His partner, Brody, nodded his head and mumbled an unintelligible reply.

Kirk made another effort to engage Brody in conversation. "Breeze is really kicking up." He figured that chatting might make the time go faster and distract him from how much he disliked heights.

Apparently, Brody didn't share Kirk's desire for chatting, for he merely said, "Yup," and kept scrubbing.

Suddenly, an extremely strong gust of wind knocked Kirk onto his hands and knees and then blew him off the platform. In horror, he found himself hanging from the scaffold by his fingertips. *Thank God for my safety harness.*

Brody lay down flat on his stomach and slid closer to Kirk. "Grab my hand!"

Kirk hesitated for only a second before letting go with his right hand and reaching for Brody. But before he could grasp his partner's hand, he heard an ominous tearing noise. The fingers of Kirk's left hand, wet with nervous perspiration, began slipping farther off the edge of the scaffold.

Taking a deep breath, he lunged awkwardly for Brody and missed. Kirk suddenly felt himself falling as gravity pulled him ruthlessly toward the ground. As he fell, he realized the horrible tearing noise he'd just heard must have been the sound of his safety harness failing.

. . . .

"Prepare for descent," Emmett said as he skillfully lowered the helicopter onto the roof of the community hospital, where our cardiac patient awaited us. Almost immediately after we landed, Emmett said, "Change in plans. We've been diverted upstate. We've got a 28-year-old fall victim. It sounds like he fell about thirty feet off a scaffold and onto the sidewalk below."

"Any information about injuries?" Julia asked, her voice crackling slightly from static.

"The patient is complaining of severe low back pain. Possible internal injuries as well. A ground unit has been dispatched to prepare the patient for transport. We'll be meeting them in a field close to the trauma location," Emmett replied.

"What happens to the cardiac patient?" I asked.

"Either another unit will pick him up or we'll swing back later today. They might even decide to send him by ground. The trauma takes priority," Julia replied.

About 45 minutes later, we began descending into a grassy meadow. I could see through the window that a blue-and-white ambulance was waiting for us at the edge of the field.

"The ambulance team will have our patient all ready to go. There aren't any regional trauma centers within driving distance from here," Lamont explained.

When Emmett gave us the go-ahead, we exited the chopper and jogged across the field toward the waiting ambulance. One of the EMS crew members stepped out of the rig and met us halfway. "We have a 28-year-old male," she said. "He fell 30 feet onto concrete and is now complaining of severe back pain and stomach pain. His vital signs are good: blood pressure 110 over 72, heart rate 86, and respiratory rate 14. His pulse ox is 98 percent on high-flow oxygen. We immobilized him with a cervical collar and spinal board."

"Excellent. Let's bring him over to the chopper." Julia pulled open the rear doors of the ambulance, and the EMS crew lifted the stretcher out into the fresh air.

"Hi, I'm Kirk," the patient introduced himself to us. "I hate heights, and I'm not a big fan of airplanes. Isn't there a certain irony to the fact that I just fell three stories and now I'm about to get into a helicopter?" Although he was obviously in a lot of pain, he managed to smile. I knew his upbeat attitude would go a long way in helping him recover.

Julia winked. "No problem. I'll tell the pilot to fly extra low for you. Just high enough to clear the cars on the highway."

Kirk looked at her suspiciously for a second (or at least he tried to look at her, which was rather challenging because he was wearing a cervical collar and was strapped to a backboard). "Well, I suppose you can fly a little higher than that."

I thought it was a good sign that he was able to joke despite the gravity of his injuries. Julia and Lamont smoothly transferred him from the ambulance stretcher to the helicopter. "I remember as I was falling I thought to myself, *Heaven help me.* I just didn't think my helpers would literally materialize out of the sky. You guys aren't actually angels, are you?"

"Well, Julia's been called an angel many times, but no, we're truly human folks," Lamont said as he established an IV line for Kirk.

"Please forgive my corny sense of humor. It helps me take my mind off the pain."

"Is it getting worse?" Julia asked with concern. "Or about the same?"

A grimace marred Kirk's face. "The same. It feels like someone stuck a pitchfork through my low back and is twisting it back and forth."

"We're going to give you something for pain right now. It should start to kick in within a few minutes," Julia said.

Kirk's vital signs remained stable throughout the trip to the trauma center, and his pain eased a bit. The time passed quickly, and before I knew it, Emmett was landing us on another hospital roof. Julia and

Lamont seamlessly transferred the care of Kirk to the awaiting trauma team. We all said our goodbyes and wished him well.

"Time to head home," Emmett said when we returned to the chopper. "How would you like to ride up front with me, Andrea?"

"I would love to!" I blurted. The next hour was perhaps one of the most splendid of my life. I watched in awe as Emmett flew us skillfully out of the city and over breathtaking mountains and trees. Just when I thought the views couldn't get any more amazing, he flew us directly over a large, majestic river.

Thank You, Lord, for the gift of this incredible day.

. . . .

He makes winds his messengers,
flames of fire his servants.

PSALM 104:4

We found out later that day that Kirk suffered a severe compression fracture of his fifth lumbar vertebra and underwent emergency surgery. I felt confident that with his youth, strength, and sense of humor, he would make an excellent recovery—although I was pretty sure he'd be exiting from the window-cleaning business. I imagined he'd find a new career that would keep him a bit more, shall I say, grounded.

26

Unresponsive but Breathing

Keep me from deceitful ways;
be gracious to me and teach me your law.

PSALM 119:29

Pine Cove Police. What is your emergency?" Dispatcher Franklin asked.

"I'm really dizzy," Lyla Throckmorton said before briefly setting the cordless phone on her coffee table to wipe her sweaty palms on her jeans.

When she picked up the phone again, she heard, "Ma'am, what's your name?"

"Lyla."

"Lyla what?"

Silence.

"Lyla, do you need an ambulance?"

"I'm dizzy."

"I'm going to send an ambulance. Where do you live?"

Silence.

. . . .

> **DISPATCHER:** "Request for first aid at the Kensington Condos, building 2, unit 1, for a female complaining of dizziness, possibly falling unconscious."

197

Buddy Stone slid into the driver's seat of the ambulance and flipped on the emergency lights. Within a minute, Jessie Barnes hopped into the front passenger seat, and Darren Williams and I climbed into the back of the rig.

"Be advised, the officer on the scene reports the patient is convulsing. Expedite," Dispatcher Franklin said.

"We're responding," Buddy replied as he pulled out onto the road and began blasting the siren.

I glanced out the window and saw a frightened squirrel scamper out onto the roadway but then turn around and rush back to the grass. By the time Darren and I had gathered the necessary equipment, we were pulling up in front of the condo complex.

The late morning sun took the chill out of the crisp autumn air. We jogged across a front lawn full of brown crunchy leaves toward building 2. As we climbed the front porch steps to unit 1, I noticed that a potted bright-yellow mum on the second step had been tipped over. As I followed Jessie into the home, I made a mental note to right the mum on our way out.

"This is Lyla Throckmorton. She just came out of a tonic-clonic seizure," Officer Sims explained. "She has a history of epilepsy. She's coming around now and doesn't want to go to the hospital. She's going to be an RMA." That meant she was refusing medical attention.

Lyla smiled apologetically. "I've had seizures since I was a child. I'm never quite sure when they're going to strike, but fortunately it's not too often. I'll call my mother to come sit with me for a bit, but I definitely don't want to go to the hospital." As she spoke, she twisted her long grayish-brown hair up into a loose bun. "Unfortunately, I'm used to this routine. I'll give my neurologist a call, just in case she wants to see me. I suppose she might want to adjust my meds or something."

While Darren checked Lyla's heart rate and blood pressure, I filled out the call sheet and prepared the refusal form. Just as Lyla was signing it, Officer McGovern walked past saying, "We've just got another call for an unresponsive male. We'll meet you there."

No sooner had he spoken than our pagers went off.

We said a quick goodbye to Lyla and reminded her that she could call us back if necessary. I regretted that I didn't have time to right the yellow mum after all. Instead, I rushed past it, and soon we were heading across town toward our next assignment.

"This was an RMA," Buddy advised dispatch. "We're heading to Clementine Road. Please have any additional responding members meet us at the scene."

"The house is on your right," Buddy called back to us. "You can jump out and get started. I'm going to back down the driveway."

I spotted a small blue ranch house with a decorative white picket fence. The screen door stood wide open, inviting us to hurry in. Darren, Jessie, and I grabbed the first aid equipment and hustled inside.

A woman with short brown hair who looked to be in her fifties met us in the front foyer. "Dad's in the back," she said, pointing toward the rear of the home. "He was watching TV and then started shaking all over. The next thing we knew, he was completely unresponsive. I called 911 right away."

We followed her through the kitchen into a cozy family room that overlooked a shady backyard with a small deck. A very frail, elderly gentleman lay unresponsive on a pullout sofa bed. His face was ashen, and his arms were bent up tight against his body. *Decorticate posturing. Not a good sign.*

"Here's what we've learned so far," Officer McGovern began. "This is Tony Wentworth. He has colon cancer, renal failure on hemodialysis, two heart blockages, and high cholesterol. He just got out of the hospital three days ago due to lethargy and hypotension after dialysis."

"Blood pressure is 86 over 44, and heart rate is 60 and strong but irregular," Officer Sims chimed in. "When we arrived, his respiratory rate was 10, but now it's only 6. I'm setting up the bag valve mask."

I pulled our oral airway kit out of our first aid bag. At a glance, our patient looked to be about a size-nine airway. I checked by measuring from the tip of his ear to the corner of his mouth. Then I carefully slid the airway into place. *No gag reflex. Another bad sign.*

Buddy poked his head into the room. "I'll grab the collapsible stretcher." We'd need it to get Tony safely from the sofa bed to our cot.

I held the BVM on Tony's face while Officer Sims squeezed it once every five seconds. I noticed that Tony was sweating profusely. The mask slid on his skin unless I held it firmly in place.

When Buddy returned with the collapsible stretcher, we worked as a team, quickly placing it underneath Tony. I couldn't help but notice how incredibly thin he was. *The colon cancer must really be taking a toll on him.*

Buddy motioned toward a door in the kitchen. "We can take him out this side door. I have the cot set up at the bottom of the porch steps."

Tony's daughter grabbed hold of his hand just before we lifted him. "Dad, it's me, Erin. Can you hear me?" Her voice quivered as she spoke. Her father remained unresponsive, seemingly unaware of his surroundings.

"Does your father have a DNR?" I asked.

"What's that?"

"A 'do not resuscitate' order," I explained. "Does he want CPR or other life-saving measures?"

Erin frowned. "I don't know. We never talked about it."

"The paramedics are still unavailable," Officer McGovern said.

I knew we'd have to continue to provide artificial respirations to help Tony's breathing, but I prayed his heart would keep beating.

The trip to the hospital was grim. Jessie, Darren and I continued to assist Tony's breathing and monitor his vital signs. As we transferred his care over to the hospital team, I knew in my heart that he'd likely reached the end of his time here on earth—if not today, then within the next couple of days.

Be with him and his family, Lord.

. . . .

The next day began with light gray, overcast skies and a gentle rain.

As morning turned to afternoon, the skies grew darker and the rain became heavier. Our pagers were silent until about half past three.

> **DISPATCHER:** "Request for first aid at 824 Hanover Road for an elderly male, unresponsive but breathing."

Another call for a person who's unresponsive but breathing, so soon after the last call? I hoped this poor gentleman would fare better than Tony Wentworth did yesterday.

I met up with Darren and Buddy at our first aid building, and we quickly took off for Hanover Road. The rain bounced off the front windshield, and I took a moment to zip up my raincoat and put on my hood.

Darren turned the windshield wipers up a notch. "It's nasty out." He pulled up in front of a brown split-level home that boasted a set of matching Colorado spruce trees in the front yard. We stepped through the front door and climbed up eight steps to the living room, where we met a couple of older women.

"I'm Margo Talbot, and this is my sister, Mildred. It's my husband, Rudy. Yesterday, he had a slight fever and the runs. He even vomited once. He said he felt better today, but an hour ago, he decided he wanted to take a nap. When I went in to check on him, I couldn't wake him up." Her voice rose an octave as she spoke, and her agitation was almost palpable. "He's in our bedroom, down the hall on the right. I'm going to call our family doctor."

I followed Buddy and Darren down a narrow hallway, past a bathroom to a dimly lit bedroom. A frail, elderly male lay very still in his bed. He wore green plaid pajamas, and a burgundy comforter was pulled up to his waist. In contrast to Tony Wentworth, Rudy looked almost peaceful.

"Rudy, can you hear me?" Buddy asked, tapping his shoulder. Rudy remained motionless. "Why don't you take his blood pressure?" he suggested, handing me a cuff.

"Mr. Talbot, I'm going to take your blood pressure," I explained, although I knew it was possible that he couldn't hear or understand me. I pumped up the cuff and slowly deflated it as I listened with my stethoscope. "Pressure's good. It's 124 over 74."

"Better than mine," Darren commented as he passed me the pulse oximeter.

After a moment, I reported, "Pulse ox is good too. It's 98 percent on room air. Heart rate is 76 and regular."

"I'll go find out more about his medical history, like if he's a diabetic," Buddy said and slipped out of the room.

I looked at my watch and studied Rudy's chest, counting his respiratory rate. "Fourteen," I said, and Darren marked it down on our call sheet.

I paused for a moment and looked at Rudy's face more closely. It seemed like his eyes were beginning to open. "Rudy, it's Andrea from the first aid squad. Can you hear me?"

Then a strange thing happened. As I peered at Rudy's face, he seemed to shut his eyes more tightly. It reminded me of a child who's pretending to sleep. Darren noticed too. We exchanged a puzzled look. "Rudy, I just saw you open your eyes. Please open them again and tell me what's going on."

One of Rudy's eyes slowly opened, and then the other popped open too. He peered slowly to the left and then to the right, as if searching the room for someone or something. "Are they here?" he whispered softly.

"Is who here?" Darren asked.

"My wife."

"No, she's in the kitchen," I replied.

His narrow shoulders relaxed slightly, and he grinned sheepishly. "Um, did my wife call you?"

"Yes, she called 911 because she couldn't wake you up. We were called because you were unresponsive."

"That's a strong word. I prefer the word 'tired.'" A guilty expression flashed across his face. He looked like the proverbial kid who had been caught with his hand in the cookie jar.

"You were tired?" Darren questioned. "So tired she couldn't wake you up?"

"It's like this," Rudy said. "I can't get any rest. The two of them have been bugging me nonstop since I got sick yesterday. 'Rudy, do you want some water? Rudy, do you want some chicken noodle soup? Rudy, did you make any more diarrhea? Rudy, Rudy, Rudy.' I couldn't take it anymore. When they came in here to check on me, I decided to pretend I was sleeping. I didn't mean to scare them or anything. I just need a little rest."

This was a first for me. Faking sleep and getting called out on it. "You know, it sounds to me like they really care about you."

"Promise you won't tell them. I'm sorry to bring you out here, but as you can plainly see, I don't need to go to the hospital. Just tell them I was sound asleep, but I woke up and I'm okay," he pleaded.

Buddy reentered the room. "No diabetes. Really not much medical history except being ill yesterday. Oh, I see he's coming around."

"You could say that," Darren said, hiding a smirk. "I think Rudy's feeling refreshed from his nap."

Somehow, Rudy managed to convince his wife and sister-in-law that he was fine and had just been sleeping heavily. He signed our refusal form, and we were on our way.

. . . .

In the year that King Uzziah died, I saw the Lord, high and exalted, seated on a throne; and the train of his robe filled the temple. Above him were seraphim, each with six wings: With two wings they covered their faces, with two they covered their feet, and with two they were flying. And they were calling to one another:

*"Holy, holy, holy is the L*ORD* Almighty;*
the whole earth is full of his glory."

ISAIAH 6:1-3

I couldn't help but compare Tony and Rudy: two frail, elderly men who were "unresponsive but breathing." I imagined seraphim were preparing to meet Tony as he approached the gates of heaven. I was glad Rudy was merely "sleeping" and didn't need our services after all. A smile lit my face, and I embraced the rain as we returned to our ambulance. *Cleansing rain. A fresh start. A new beginning.*

27

Small Town Community

*Let us consider how we may spur one another
on toward love and good deeds,
not giving up meeting together,
as some are in the habit of doing,
but encouraging one another—
and all the more as you see
the Day approaching.*

HEBREWS 10:24-25

'd love to join your squad," an older gentleman with snow-white hair said as he reached out to shake my hand. "My name is Lewis Bernes. It's a pleasure to meet you."

I discreetly tried to wipe some cookie crumbs off my lips (I'm a bit of a dessert hound) as I smiled and returned Lewis's handshake. Our church had held a special service to honor the local police, firefighters, and EMS personnel. Now we were gathered in the community room, enjoying light refreshments and fellowship.

"We'd love to have you join." I launched into a detailed description of what's involved in becoming a volunteer. Rescue squads are always eager to recruit new members.

Lewis seemed intrigued. I explained that since we live in a small town, we're able to respond to the building when our pagers are activated, rather than waiting at the building for a first aid call.

"I'll give it some serious thought. My concern is that I'm too old. I may not look it, but I'm pushing 80."

"We have lots of members who are senior citizens. They're a huge help in answering daytime calls when our younger members are at work or school."

I took down his name and information and promised to mail him an application within the next few days.

· · · · · · · · · · · · · ·

One year later

> **DISPATCHER:** "Request for first aid at 614 Hanover Road for an elderly male who is not feeling well."

Archie Harris, Ted O'Malley, and I knocked on the front door of a cozy cottage close to the beach. Sergeant Flint quickly opened the door. "The patient is in the back bedroom," he said, turning around and leading the way.

When I entered the room, much to my surprise, I saw Lewis Bernes perched on the edge of his bed. He managed a smile when he saw us. "I'm glad you came. Do you remember me?"

"Of course. I met you at the service for first responders. I'm sorry I'm not seeing you again under better circumstances." I felt his forehead and noted that it felt hot to the touch.

"I'm really sorry I never sent back the application to join the squad. I filled it out, but I never mailed it. My brother got sick, and now I take care of him."

"It's okay. I knew something must have come up." I wrapped the blood pressure cuff around his upper arm.

"Well, I just wanted you to know that I didn't forget about you. I really did want to join."

I gently steered the conversation to what had prompted Mr. Bernes to call us.

"I've been sick for two days. Fever, dry cough, chills. I haven't been able to eat, and I think it's throwing off my sugar level. I'm a diabetic."

"Have you checked your sugar today?"

"I took it just before I called. It's 54. I took my insulin earlier today, but maybe I shouldn't have." It's common for us to be dispatched for diabetic emergencies when people take their usual insulin dose, but either eat less food or burn off more energy than usual for some reason.

"Well, you look like you need to get checked out at the hospital. The ER doc will sort all that out," Archie said.

"That's exactly what I was thinking," Mr. Bernes replied. "I'd try to eat something now, but I'm simply not up to it. I tried to eat a sandwich, but it tasted like sawdust, and I started to get nauseated. I really wish I could stay home and look after my brother, but I know I need to go. My sister is coming over to look after him. Fortunately, he's sleeping right now. I don't think he's even aware that you're all here."

After finishing our assessment, we assisted Mr. Bernes onto our stair chair and then out to our ambulance. A short time later, we dropped him off at the emergency department at Bakersville Hospital. I gave him a quick hug and wished him well. I hoped he'd be home and feeling well soon.

. . . .

Eight months later

> **DISPATCHER:** "Request for first aid at 614 Hanover Road for a person with an anxiety attack."

The address sounded familiar. I knew I'd been there before. When Archie, Ted, and I pulled up in front of a small yellow cottage, I realized with dismay that it was Lewis Bernes's home. I recalled that he'd mentioned his brother was ill. I wondered if our first aid call was for Lewis or his brother.

The yellow-tinted porch light illuminated the brick walkway. The front door was slightly ajar, so I knocked lightly before stepping inside.

I spotted Lewis right away. He was seated at a beech-wood kitchen table with a white tile top. Officer Endicott stood at the kitchen counter, gathering up medication bottles. "This is Lewis Bernes. He thinks he's having an anxiety attack."

"Hi, Mr. Bernes. It's Andrea. I met you at the—"

"Church. I remember. Thanks for coming."

"What's going on tonight?" I noticed his untouched dinner sat on the place mat in front of him.

"I feel funny. I've been under a lot of stress. I think I'm having an anxiety attack."

"Have you ever had one before?" I asked, slipping my fingers onto his wrist to check his radial pulse. It was strong and regular, with a rate of 70. More often when we see patients with anxiety attacks, their pulse is rapid (over 100).

"No, but I've had a terrible couple of weeks. Two weeks ago, my brother passed away. Then this morning, we buried my sister. I'm the only one left now."

"I'm so sorry," I said. His grief was almost palpable, and I fervently wished I could ease some of his pain. "Mr. Bernes, I remember from the last time I saw you that you have diabetes. Have you eaten today?"

Lewis looked thoughtful for a moment. "No, I guess not. I just wasn't up to it. I did heat that up," he said, pointing to the microwave dinner in front of him, "but I just didn't have the heart to eat it."

"When was your last meal?" Archie asked.

"Well, I ate half of a bagel for breakfast yesterday."

"It sounds like the first thing you need to do is eat," Ted said. "Your blood sugar is probably low." He picked up Lewis's blood-glucose meter from the counter and placed it in front of him. Lewis pricked his finger and placed a drop of blood on the test strip, then placed the strip into the meter. "Forty-six."

"I know you don't feel up to eating, but we really need to get some food in you," I said, pushing the dinner closer to him. "If this is too cold, I can pop it back in the microwave."

"It's okay." He slowly ate some bites of beef, mashed potatoes, and broccoli. I poured him a glass of orange juice to help further raise his blood sugar level. When he finished eating, he rechecked his sugar. "Eighty-seven."

"Much better," Ted said. "But you'll have to keep a close eye on it."

"Would you like to go to the hospital to get checked out?" I asked, guessing that he would prefer to stay home. After such an emotionally exhausting day, I figured the last thing he'd want to do would be to spend the night in the emergency room.

"I'll pass. I should have known it was my diabetes acting up. It's been such a terrible day, I just assumed I was feeling anxious."

"Can I call someone to stay with you?" Officer Endicott asked. "It might be better to have someone keep an eye on you tonight."

"You could call my niece, Sheila. Her phone number is on the fridge."

I carefully prepared a refusal form for him to sign. "How are you feeling now?"

"Better. Much better. I don't feel nearly so jittery anymore. I think I just need some rest." After Lewis signed the release form, we all shook hands with him.

. . . .

The angel said to me, "These words are trustworthy and true. The Lord, the God who inspires the prophets, sent his angel to show his servants the things that must soon take place."

REVELATION 22:6

As emergency responders, we often are called to help people at their most vulnerable moments. I knew that Lewis was a Christ-loving man, and I felt confident that the Lord would carry him through this time of sadness. I prayed that the angels of the Lord would bring him comfort.

28

The Holiday Miracle

*I am like an olive tree
flourishing in the house of God;
I trust in God's unfailing love
for ever and ever.
For what you have done I will always praise you
in the presence of your faithful people.
And I will hope in your name,
for your name is good.*

PSALM 52:8-9

The pain was excruciating. It radiated from Oliver Overton's left hip, up his back and down his leg. He knew he was in serious trouble. When he'd fallen in his bedroom a few hours ago, he'd landed hard on his left side. He had managed to roll off his painful hip and onto his back, but that was as far as he could get. Now he could see from the light beams sneaking in his window that the sun was beginning to rise.

It seems like only yesterday that I was running marathons. Now I can't even walk from my bathroom to my bedroom without falling. Why didn't I use my walker? Why didn't I ever get one of those things that you wear around your neck and has a button to press for help if you get into trouble?

Hours passed. Oliver was dimly aware that he was becoming hungry when he heard his stomach growl loudly. He started growing thirsty too. He began dreaming of a nice steaming-hot cup of coffee with milk and just a hint of sugar. The hard wood floor was uncomfortable, and the cold seemed to seep directly into his bones.

Gradually, the bedroom grew darker. *A whole day has passed by. When will anyone notice I'm here?* The thought chilled him. He didn't have any family. He had good neighbors, but he didn't speak to them every day. He knew they might not realize something was amiss until it was too late.

Oliver found himself reflecting on his life. He'd been blessed with a fantastic marriage. His dear wife had passed away five years ago, and he still missed her deeply. They'd tried for years to have children, but after numerous miscarriages, they'd finally accepted that it was not in their future. With a strong love for Christ, they had focused their energy on establishing a charity for children with cancer.

The sun set and rose again. The pain was becoming almost unbearable. *How many days and nights have I lain on this floor? Dear Lord, I have been Your humble servant for all these years. If it be Your will, please save me from this suffering.*

· · · · · · · · · · · · · ·

Using her wooden rake as a weapon, Victoria Quincy attacked the brown oak leaves that lurked under her holly bushes with gusto. She waged war on them, ruthlessly pushing her rake underneath the bushes again and again, as far as she could reach, lest one of the leaves somehow escape.

Satisfied at last, she glanced at her watch. Her husband, Herb, was due home any minute. The two planned to enjoy lunch together in their three-season room. With Thanksgiving just around the corner and winter fast approaching, she knew their time to enjoy the sunroom was nearly coming to an end for the year. Today, even though it was quite sunny, there was a distinct autumn chill in the air, hinting at the coming winter.

With a smile of contentment, Victoria leaned back on her heels to survey her garden. It looked neat and tidy now, and she was glad she could see her lawn again instead of just an endless sea of brown, crunchy leaves. Her yard wasn't particularly big, but she felt that it was just the right size for a 63-year-old like herself. In the spring, she planted annuals and a small garden of grape tomatoes, cucumbers, lettuce, and green peppers. In the summer, she enjoyed picking fresh blueberries and watching the birds splash in the birdbath. In the fall, she battled the endless sea of leaves. She loved every second of it. Since her children were grown and living on their own now, she had plenty of extra time to spend in her yard.

Victoria took off her gardening gloves and leaned her rake on the wall just inside her garage door, where it would be within easy reach for the next time. She strolled a short distance to her rear patio door and stepped into her cozy family room. She took a moment to straighten a few knickknacks on her fireplace mantel and a small landscape painting that always seemed to tilt slightly off center.

As she headed toward the kitchen, an odd sensation swept over her. Before she could even react, she collapsed onto the family room floor. Her heart stopped beating, and she was no longer breathing.

Victoria Quincy was clinically dead.

. . . .

Herb Quincy parked in the garage and fished his house key out of his pocket. He and Victoria always kept their house locked for security reasons. He was a retired correctional officer, and even though they lived in a safe neighborhood, he felt like one could never be too cautious.

"Honey, I'm home," he called out as he unlocked the door. He knew that Victoria would already have their lunches prepared, because they always ate at 12 o'clock on the nose. When she didn't answer, he figured she may have lost track of time and could still be out in the garden.

As Herb rounded the corner from the mudroom into the family room, he was horrified to find his wife lying motionless, spread-eagled on the family room floor. "Victoria!" he cried out as he rushed to her side. Frantically, he rolled her from her stomach onto her back. Her jaw hung open, and her eyes had a dull, fixed stare. Rushing to the telephone, Herb dialed 911.

· · · · · · · · · · · · ·

DISPATCHER: "Request for first aid at 1411 Wesley Avenue for a 63-year-old woman who is unresponsive and not breathing. Family member is starting to perform CPR."

· · · · · · · · · · · · ·

Oliver Overton drifted into an uncomfortable sleep but roused at the sound of distant police sirens. *Thank God! Help is finally on the way.* Relief flooded through him as the sound of the sirens drew closer and closer. His hearing wasn't what it used to be, but he listened anxiously for the sound of his doorbell. However, the house remained ominously silent, and eventually he had to face the sad realization that no one was there to rescue him after all.

· · · · · · · · · · · · ·

"We're responding to 1411 Wesley Avenue," Archie Harris told the dispatcher as Meg Potter, Ted O'Malley, and I scrambled to grab all the equipment necessary for a CPR call. With sirens wailing, we arrived a few minutes later in front of a dark-brown Victorian with decorative white trim running along the length of the front porch. I was too focused on the first aid call to pay much attention to the immaculate front lawn or the spectacular arrangement of colorful mums in the garden bed.

The four of us rushed through the foyer and off to the right, into the family room. Sergeant Flint was kneeling next to a middle-aged woman and performing vigorous chest compressions, while Officer Endicott was delivering rescue breaths with a bag valve mask.

"We don't have much information yet, other than her name—Victoria Quincy. Her husband, Herb, is on the phone in the kitchen," Officer Endicott said.

I thought the woman looked young to be in cardiac arrest. Her face, though smooth of wrinkles, was an unnatural shade of bluish-purple, indicating she'd been without oxygen for some time.

As Ted and Meg began assisting the police, I grabbed our patient clipboard and retraced my steps to the kitchen, where I found a distraught gentleman speaking on the phone.

"I came home and found your mom lying on the floor, and she wouldn't wake up. I called 911 right away. The dispatcher told me how to do CPR." Herb was silent for a few seconds and then said, "No. She's not breathing right now. Listen, the EMTs are here and one of them wants to speak with me. I'll see you at the hospital. I need you to call your brothers and sisters and let them know what's going on. I love you." He turned to me, his eyes bright with unshed tears.

"Sir, may I ask you some questions? When did you last see your wife?"

"Two hours ago. She was going outside to rake the leaves, and I left to run some errands."

"Did she say anything about not feeling well?"

Herb tugged nervously at the cuff of his shirt sleeve. "No, not a word. I think she would've told me if she didn't feel good. And she wouldn't have gone out to do yard work."

"What kind of past medical history does your wife have?" I asked, carefully jotting down everything he said onto the patient report.

"Just high blood pressure. It's controlled with medication, though."

"Can you tell me what medications she takes?" I felt bad asking him so many questions when he was obviously upset, but the information was vital.

"Just one for blood pressure. I'll have to look in our medicine cabinet to get the name of it for you."

"Does she have any allergies to medications?"

Herb scratched his head. "None that I know of. You'll have to excuse me. I feel like I'm in shock. Like I'm in some terrible nightmare."

"I'm so sorry," I said, but the words sounded woefully inadequate. I asked him a few more questions, like his wife's date of birth, before returning to the family room. Unfortunately, Victoria still looked the same: pulseless and apneic (not breathing).

"We shocked her twice, but still no pulse. We're about ready to try again now," Ted said.

Meg pressed the analyze button on the defibrillator, and I held my breath as it announced, "Shock advised." Meg pressed the shock button, and I watched as the joules of energy from the defibrillator made Victoria's body jerk.

"No pulse. Continue CPR," Ted said.

I swallowed my disappointment and busied myself by pushing our stretcher closer to Victoria. She was already on a backboard, so after Archie finished a set of chest compressions, Sergeant Flint and Officer Endicott lifted her up onto the cot. They rolled the stretcher out the front door and lifted it down three small front porch steps, while Archie and Meg did their best to continue performing CPR.

As I paused to grab our first aid bag, a woman in her late forties wearing a floral dress rushed up and grabbed my arm. "What's wrong with Victoria? I'm her neighbor Peggy."

"We're taking her to the hospital right now." I knew I was stating the obvious, but I really couldn't give more information than that due to privacy concerns. "Why don't you go inside and ask her husband if there is anything you can do to help?"

"Thanks. I'll do that right now." Peggy rushed past me and disappeared into the house. By the time I caught up with the rest of my crew, they had already loaded Victoria into the back of our ambulance, and paramedics Rose Anderson and William Moore were assessing her.

"V-fib," Rose said as she looked at Victoria's rhythm on the heart monitor. "Everyone clear. I'm going to shock."

I held my breath as Rose placed defibrillation paddles on Victoria's chest and administered a shock.

"I have a strong carotid. Hold compressions and continue with rescue breathing," William said as he prepared his equipment to intubate Victoria.

I picked up our portable suction unit from the floor and placed it on the ambulance's counter in case we needed it again. Victoria still looked awfully pale, though not nearly as blue anymore. I hoped she didn't have anoxic brain damage.

It seemed as though Victoria was trying to take a few breaths on her own, which was certainly an encouraging sign. Meg stepped out of our ambulance to drive the paramedics' rig so Rose and William could continue to provide advanced life support.

Sergeant Flint opened the side door. "You can go. Herb's going to drive his car and meet you at the hospital."

Victoria's heart continued beating the entire way to Bakersville Hospital, where we left her in the capable hands of Dr. Morgan and her team of emergency room personnel. As I moved out of Victoria's room, I looked back one last time. *Please help her and keep her safe, Lord.*

. . . .

One day later

Rowena London snapped a collar and leash around her small Yorkshire terrier and led him outside. She walked Chipper four or five times a day, and she wasn't sure who enjoyed the fresh air and exercise more. Sometimes she drove to the park or beach for their walk, but today she decided to simply walk around the block.

Rowena walked slowly down the street, pausing to give Chipper a chance to sniff a tree. Then they rounded the corner and leisurely strolled along the next block. As Chipper paused at a fire hydrant, Rowena studied a small gray split-level home. The shades were drawn, and she noticed that several newspapers were lying on the front porch.

Tugging gently on Chipper's leash, she led him up the walkway and onto the little front porch. She rang the doorbell, and when there was no response after several minutes, she rang it again. She stood indecisively for a moment, then glanced behind her and noticed that mail was sticking out of the mailbox.

Rowena decided to return home. When she arrived, she called the nonemergency number of the Pine Cove Police Department.

"Hi. This is Rowena London. I was wondering if one of your officers could come and check a house around the corner from mine. The owner's not answering the door, and his newspapers are piling up."

She was relieved when the dispatcher said he would send an officer right away. She hated to be an alarmist, but she would never forgive herself if something was wrong with the person who lived there. After quickly patting Chipper on the head, she rushed back outside to see if she could assist the police officers at the home.

....

We were just heading back to our first aid building after bringing an oncology patient with trouble breathing to the emergency room when our pagers went off again.

> **DISPATCHER:** "Request for first aid at 587 Hudson Avenue for a 90-year-old man with weakness, dehydration, and a possible hip fracture. Patient appears to have been lying on the floor for several days."

Meg frowned. "Two or three days is an awfully long time for an elderly person to lie on the floor, especially with a broken hip."

A few minutes later, we pulled up in front of a light-gray, clapboard split-level house. We found our patient, Oliver Overton, with Sergeant Flint on the second floor in the master bedroom.

"Good thing your neighbor called to have us come check on you, Mr. Overton," Sergeant Flint said. He took a few steps back to give Meg room to perform an assessment.

"Amen," Oliver said, his voice sounding weak and raspy. "I'm not sure how much longer I could have hung on."

I reflected on the full impact of what had transpired. If Oliver's neighbor hadn't taken the time to call the police, no one would have discovered that something was amiss until it was possibly too late.

....

Two days later, we learned that Oliver underwent a surgical repair of his hip fracture and was recovering well. Victoria Quincy was still clinging to life, but she remained unresponsive and was hooked up to a ventilator.

About three weeks passed. One day, Ted and I were in the first aid building, cleaning up after a call. We'd left the garage door open to let in some crisp, fresh air. A gray sedan pulled up onto our concrete apron in front of the building.

"Better see what they want," Ted said. "They probably need directions somewhere."

After putting away an oxygen tank, I stepped from our garage area into the bright sunlight and blinked several times. A middle-aged couple stepped out of the car. They looked familiar, but I couldn't quite place them.

"Hello," the woman said. "I asked my husband to drive over here so I could thank you. He told me all about how your squad and the police department helped me several weeks ago."

My pulse suddenly quickened with hope, and I peered at the woman and gentleman more closely. "Are you Mrs. Quincy?"

The megawatt smile that she beamed in reply answered my question. I closed the distance between us and hugged her tightly. "You look wonderful!" I exclaimed with amazement.

"Yes, better than the last time you saw her," Herb quipped.

"I was incredibly blessed to be able to come home a few days ago. Now I'm looking forward to celebrating the Christmas season."

. . . .

I was left alone, gazing at this great vision; I had no strength left, my face turned deathly pale and I was helpless. Then I heard him speaking, and as I listened to him, I fell into a deep sleep, my face to the ground.

A hand touched me and set me trembling on my hands and knees. He said, "Daniel, you who are highly esteemed, consider carefully the words I am about to speak to you, and stand up, for I have now been sent to you." And when he said this to me, I stood up trembling.

Then he continued, "Do not be afraid, Daniel. Since the first day that you set your mind to gain understanding and to humble

yourself before your God, your words were heard, and I have
come in response to them."

DANIEL 10:8-12

In Revelation 19:10; 22:8-9; and Colossians 2:18, we are
reminded to worship God, not angels. However, we can
acknowledge their role in our lives as protectors and strengtheners. Under the direction of God, angels may answer our prayers,
rescue us from danger, provide for our needs, and care for us at
the moment of our death. We may be receptive to their presence in our lives and appreciate their role as God's ministers.

In the case of Mrs. Quincy, I gave thanks to God for rescu-
ing her and letting her continue her life on earth with her family. *Thank You, Lord. A true holiday miracle!*

About the Author

Andrea Jo Rodgers has been a volunteer EMT for more than 30 years and has responded to more than 8,000 first aid and fire calls. She holds a clinical doctorate in physical therapy and has worked as a physical therapist in a trauma center for 25 years.

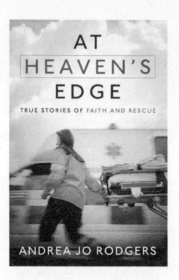

911... What Is Your Emergency?

Veteran EMT Andrea Rodgers has helped hundreds of people in their most vulnerable moments.

Some of the victims faced their mortality head-on and cried out to God for help. Many experienced fleeting but life-changing connections with their first responders. Often these crises became unexpected sources of inspiration.

Now Andrea shares brief, real-life stories of heroic courage in the face of fear. In times of intense suffering, she has repeatedly witnessed signs of God's quiet intervention and healing presence.

- A man is resuscitated after Andrea was able to repair a defibrillator—with her teeth!
- Several bystanders help rescue a young girl who is accidently buried alive in sand.
- Andrea also experienced some lighthearted moments, including the time she arrived at the scene of a crime only to find herself in the middle of a mystery dinner theater.

Experience the miracles and life-and-death drama as you look at life from heaven's edge.

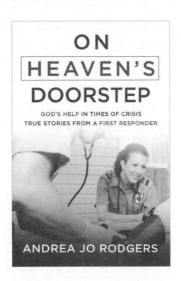

In Life or Death, There's Only One Guarantee—God Will Be There

Medical emergencies are among life's most unexpected and terrifying realities. But isn't it reassuring in times of crisis that you can find hope and comfort in the hands of a loving God?

Encounter heart-stopping drama in these real-life stories of everyday people like you who found themselves on heaven's doorstep—fully dependent on the skilled and courageous efforts of first responders and on the mercy of God.

As you read these firsthand accounts of perilous situations with uncertain outcomes, you will experience a full spectrum of emotions, from tender heartache to tremendous joy. Through it all, you will witness God's amazing love and care for His children, both for those who are brought back from the edge and for those He welcomes into eternal fellowship with Him.

Be inspired as you go on call with veteran EMT Andrea Jo Rodgers and other brave professionals dedicated to helping when humanity is at its most frail.